CHRISTMAS REFLECTIONS

Christmas Reflections

from

JAMES W. MOORE
REGINALD MALLETT
J. ELLSWORTH KALAS
JAMES A. HARNISH
NELL W. MOHNEY

DIMENSIONS
FOR LIVING
NASHVILLE

CHRISTMAS REFLECTIONS FROM JAMES W. MOORE, REGINALD MALLETT,
J. ELLSWORTH KALAS, JAMES A. HARNISH, NELL W. MOHNEY

This book is printed on acid-free paper.

ISBN 0-687-09853-X

This book is a compilation of different versions of previously published works. *What Can
We Learn from the Christ Child? An Advent Study for Adults*, by James W. Moore. Copyright
© 1997 by Abingdon Press. *The Cradle and the Star: An Advent Study for Adults*, by
Reginald Mallett. Copyright © 1996 by Abingdon Press. *The Christmas People: An Advent
Study for Adults*, by J. Ellsworth Kalas. Copyright © 1998 by Abingdon Press. *Come Home
for Christmas: An Advent Study for Adults*, by James A. Harnish. Copyright © 1999 by
Abingdon Press. *Advent: A Calendar of Devotions 1999*, by Nell W. Mohney. Copyright ©
1999 by Abingdon Press.

Scripture quotations, unless otherwise noted, are from the New Revised Standard Version
of the Bible, copyright © 1989, by the Division of Christian Education of the National
Council of the Churches of Christ in the United States of America. Used by permission.
All rights reserved.

Those noted KJV are from the King James Version of the Bible.

Those noted RSV are from the Revised Standard Version of the Bible, copyright 1946, 1952,
1971 by the Division of Christian Education of the National Council of the Churches of
Christ in the USA. Used by permission. All rights reserved.

That noted NIV is from the *Holy Bible: New International Version*. Copyright © 1973,
1978, 1984 by the International Bible Society. Used by permission of Zondervan Bible
Publishers. All rights reserved.

Those noted The Message are from *The Message*, published by NavPress, copyright © by
Eugene Peterson, 1993, 1994, 1995.

Poetry of G. K. Chesterton on pages 127, 129, 135, 143, and 150 is from "The House of
Christmas." Used with permission by A. P. Watt Ltd. on behalf of the Royal Literary Fund.

01 02 03 04 05 06 07 08 09 10—10 9 8 7 6 5 4 3 2 1

MANUFACTURED IN THE UNITED STATES OF AMERICA

CONTENTS

INTRODUCTION

Two memory vignettes formed in my mind when I finished reading this anthology, *Christmas Reflections,* by four distinguished authors. One memory was of an incident that happened on the first of many trips to the Holy Land with members from our church. Though I had believed in the Incarnation since I first came to faith as a teenager, the confirmation of it came to me on a cold, clear, star-studded night in Shepherd's Field near Bethlehem.

We were standing near the caves where the twentieth-century shepherds slept for protection from the cold and from wild animals. Those men looked as if they as if they could have been the very same shepherds who heard the angelic chorus announcing the birth of Jesus. Research tells us that shepherds in the Middle East have worn the same kind of clothing, with little variation, through the centuries. As our soloist sang "O Holy Night," I suddenly knew in my inner being that the great God of the universe had indeed come to earth at a particular time and place in the person of a baby—God's only son, Jesus the Christ. It was a defining moment in my understanding of the magnitude of God's love for us.

The second vignette was the memory of a seatmate on a flight from Florida to Tennessee one hot, July afternoon. He was a nattily dressed, silver-haired New Yorker who told me he was celebrating Christmas that day. "Christmas in July?" I asked in amazement. Then he told me that he had been a big-time gambler in New York City. On an evening of boredom and on a dare from a fellow gambler, he and three of his cronies had gone to a Billy Graham Crusade in Madison Square Garden. "I went to scoff, but I stayed to pray," he said solemnly. "My life has never been the same, and today is my spiritual birthday." Though it had been seven years since that incident occurred, the man spoke with deep emotion. Words from the Phillips Brooks Christmas carol "O Little Town of Bethlehem" flashed into my mind:

How silently, how silently,
The wondrous gift is given;
So God imparts to human hearts
The blessings of his heaven.

Those are the two facts that the four authors in this collection bring to the readers: the Incarnation of God through Christ into our world; and, if we allow it, the same Incarnation into our individual lives.

These talented authors give practical and beautiful applications of what these facts mean to us in our contemporary culture. They allow us to see the immanence and the transcendence of God through the eyes of the Holy Family and other participants in the first Christmas; through the cradle and the star; through persons in today's world who need the Christmas message of hope; and through our basic need to come home for Christmas—both physically and spiritually. These authors will inspire your thinking and touch you in the deep places of your soul. You will find yourself giving thanks that the Incarnation means "God is with us." We are never alone! *Christmas Reflections* will enable you to have a more worthy celebration of this wonderful season. I pray that it will bless your life as it has mine.

Nell W. Mohney

REFLECTION

Nell W. Mohney

nd she brought forth her first-born son and wrapped him in swaddling clothes, and laid him in a manger; because there was no room for them in the inn.
—Luke 2:7 KJV

The message of Christmas is often mixed. We are like the children, now grown, of friends of ours. Our friends were remembering a time when their son, John, was four years old and their daughter, Mary, was two. John loved seeing the television show featuring Roy Rogers and his horse, Trigger. He was equally fascinated by the story of Mary, Joseph, and the baby Jesus.

For Christmas John received a toy six-shooter, and his sister got a doll. A few days later, their mother overheard the four-year-old say to his sister: "Mary, swaddle that baby and jump on Trigger, 'cause we're heading to Bethlehem!"

Sometimes the enormousness of God's gift in Christ is lost to us amid crowded malls, too many social events, overspending, overeating, or just plain fatigue.

When we are tempted to feel that Christmas is too

commercialized, let us stop and give thanks that people who never enter a church are hearing the story of Jesus' birth through Christmas carols. When we are irritated by the traffic, we should stop and think how marvelous it is that a baby born two thousand years ago in the Middle East can cause a traffic jam halfway around the world in our city or community. The secret, of course, is to keep our eyes on Jesus, to stay focused so that his life and message tower over the confusion.

Instead of blaming others for the commercialization of Christmas, we ought to allow this question to penetrate our hearts: Is there room in my life for Jesus?

PART ONE

What Can We Learn from the Christ Child?

James W. Moore

INTRODUCTION

nce, as I was rushing through an airport, I saw a young man wearing a T-shirt with these words on the front: "Been there! Done that! Got the T-shirt!"

Unfortunately, this is the way some people approach Christmas. They've been there before, and so they approach the season with a sense of boredom—maybe even a little dread—and a sense of anxious urgency like that expressed in a country song that was popular some years ago: "If we make it through December..."

Some people see Christmas as the same old routine. They've been there, done that, got the T-shirt. They don't really expect anything new or different or exciting to happen—just long lines, traffic jams, frayed nerves, and big bills to pay.

With that in mind, let me share the legend of the touchstone. It's a good Christmas parable for us. According to the legend, if you found the touchstone on the coast of the Black Sea and held it in your hand, everything you touched would turn to gold. You would recognize the touchstone by its warmth. The other stones would feel cold, but the touchstone would turn warm in your hand.

Once a man sold everything he had, went to the Black Sea, and began picking up stones, hoping to find the touchstone. After some days passed, he realized he was picking up the same stones again and again. So he devised a plan: Pick up a stone; if it's cold, throw it into the sea. This he did for weeks and weeks.

One morning he picked up a stone. It was cold, so he threw it into the sea. He picked up another. It too felt cold, so he threw it into the sea—and so on and so on. Then he picked up yet another stone. It turned warm in his hand; but before he realized what he was doing, he threw it into the sea! He had the touchstone in his hand, and he threw it away. So dulled by the routine, he didn't recognize its specialness. Absentmindedly, he tossed it aside.

This can happen to us at Christmastime. If we are not careful, we miss the uniqueness, the power, the sacredness of the season; and before we even realize what we are doing, we throw it away, toss it aside.

In what follows, we will look at some of the special lessons Christmas can teach us, in the hope—and with the prayer—that Christmas can be for us this year what God meant it to be: the incredible gift of his amazing grace. Then, as Henry Van Dyke suggested, we can "keep Christmas" all year round.

1
What Can We Learn from Mary?

based on Luke 1:26-38; 2:1-7

A friend of mine who is a psychologist told me that he has found the perfect formula for getting through Christmas. "You just put your mind in neutral," he said, "and go where you are shoved!" Of course, he was joking, but we know full well what he was talking about. The Christmas rush, the hectic pace, the heavy traffic, the long lines, the frayed nerves, the bills, the deadlines—all these pressures cause some people to "stonewall" through the season. They just put their minds in neutral and go where they are shoved because they are overwhelmed by the stress of it all.

Please don't let that happen to you! Don't just endure the season. Enjoy it, relish it, savor it, celebrate it. Share the joy of Christmas with others, and learn from it. Christmas has so much to teach us. Take Mary, for example. She has so much to teach us about real faith. When we see her beautifully portrayed in Christmas pageants and on Christmas cards and in nativity scenes, she looks so serene and lovely.

But think about it realistically for a moment. Consider what Mary was going through. She was about to become an unwed mother. She and Joseph were engaged, but they were not married. They had not been physically intimate—and yet here she was pregnant. It must have been incredibly difficult: the whisperings behind her back, the pointed fingers, the false accusations, the raised eyebrows, the questions, the gossip, the criticism, the family pressures, the crude jokes, the cruel laughter—not to mention the poverty, the heavy taxes, and the long, hard journey mandated at a time when an expectant mother shouldn't have had to travel anywhere. Add to that giving birth in a stable, with no doctor, no midwife, no medicine or anesthetic—nothing but faith in God!

Mary was just a teenage girl from a poor family who lived in an obscure village in a tiny nation, which itself was under subjugation to a despised foreign power. Then one day—out of the blue—an angel came to her with a message from the Lord: "Do not be afraid, Mary, for you have found favor with God. And now, you will conceive in your womb and bear a son, and you will name him Jesus. He will be great, and will be called the Son of the Most High, and the Lord God will give to him the throne of his ancestor David" (Luke 1:30-32).

All this was going to happen without her ever having been intimate with any man. Now, be honest. Would you have believed that? The remarkable thing is that Mary did! That's real faith, isn't it? She was willing to hear God's Word, obey God's will, and entrust the future into God's hands—even though it put her in an awkward, difficult, and complicated situation.

How would she explain this? How would she communicate this to her parents? How would she tell Joseph? They were legally engaged. They had not yet consummated their marriage, but were considered "as good as married." In those days, once you became formally engaged, the only way you could be separated was through divorce. How could she tell Joseph, and how would he handle it? What would the neighbors say?

It was a touch situation for Mary. Under similar circumstances, most of us would have asked the Lord to find some- one else to do the job. But not Mary. Her answer to the angel was a model of real faith: "Here I am, the servant of the Lord; let it be with me according to your word" (Luke 1:38). In Mary we see a powerful portrait of faith painted with three bold strokes. Let us consider each of these, one by one.

Mary's Faith Was Great Because
She Heard God's Voice

Mary was tuned in to God. Because she was listening with the ears of faith, she was able to hear God's message and respond.

I'm convinced that God is speaking loud and clear today. Unfortunately, few of us are tuned in to hear him. Many of us get so caught up in the hectic pace of living that we stop listening. We are so inundated by the many voices and appeals in our noisy world that we pull back into a hard shell and stonewall our way through life. Too many of us "throw in the towel," retreat from the struggle, and give in to the sin of narrow-mindedness. We don't want our thoughts disturbed by new ideas, so we tune out. We have ears, but we do not listen and do not hear.

In the year 1870, a group of Methodists were gathered on a college campus. The president of the college addressed the assembly and remarked that they were living in an excit- ing age. He said that he thought they would see things hap- pen in their lifetime that seemed unbelievable to them now.

The leader of the group, a bishop, was intrigued by the col- lege president's remarks. The bishop interrupted him and asked what kinds of things he was talking about. The presi- dent of the college replied that he believed they were coming

17

into a time of great inventions. For example, he believed that one day soon they would be able to fly through the air like birds. The bishop was shocked by this, calling it a ridiculous idea and heresy. The Bible, he said, tells us that flight is reserved for the angels alone. Then he declared that there would be no more such talk.

A few days later, that same bishop, whose last name was Wright, went home to his wife and two small sons, whose names just happened to be Wilbur and Orville! The bishop had tuned out. He just wasn't listening.

A few years ago, our family gathered at Christmas for a family reunion. A month or so before our gathering, my sister Susie had given birth to her third child, a beautiful baby girl named Julie. Most of us were seeing Julie for the first time, and there was a lot of excitement about this new addition to our family. Toward evening, we put the baby in a bassinet in the back bedroom of the house. The travel and excitement had tired her out. She fell asleep immediately.

We had our Christmas dinner, and afterwards we exchanged gifts. Then everyone got involved in a variety of activities. Some were talking and visiting. Some were playing electronic games. Others were singing carols. Still others were watching a football game on television. There was a lot of noise and happy Christmas confusion. In the midst of all the chaos, I watched my sister quietly slip out of the room. Where do you think she was going? She was going to check on the baby. She had heard the baby cry out.

Isn't that something? In all the commotion, no one else heard the baby. But she did, because she was tuned in to hear the baby. She was listening for the baby. Her ears were trained to hear her baby's cry. That was her number one priority.

In the same way, Mary was tuned in to hear God. One of the great questions of Christmas is this: Are you tuned in to hear God? Above all the chaos, can you hear God? Is that a priority for you? Or have you closed your mind and shut the voice of God out of your life? Mary's faith was great because she heard God's voice.

Mary's Faith Was Great Because She Obeyed God's Will

In the original Greek of the New Testament, the word for faith is *pistis*. It literally means "believing obedience," or believing in God so much that we commit ourselves—body, mind, and soul—to the doing of God's will, come what may.

In one "Peanuts" comic strip, Linus, the statistician for Charlie Brown's baseball team, brings Charlie his final report. "I've compiled the statistics on our baseball team for this last season," Linus says. "In twelve games, we almost scored a run. In nine games, the other team almost didn't score before the first out. In right field, Lucy almost caught three balls and once almost made the right play." And then Linus says: "Charlie Brown, we led the league in 'Almost.'" That's the way many people are in regard to obeying God's will. They lead the league in "almost"! They almost obey God's will, but not quite.

Many years ago, when the great missionary David Livingstone was serving in Africa, he sent an appeal to England for more workers to come and help him with his mission work. The answer that came back from England was that they would like to send workers to help, but first they needed to know if there was a good road to the outpost. David Livingstone is said to have responded: "If you are offering to send workers who will come only if the road is easy, I can't use them. Tell them to stay home."

One of the foremost Christians of this century was William Barclay, a prolific writer of Bible commentaries and a renowned Scottish theologian and teacher. He died a few years ago at the age of eighty-five. Not long after his funeral, one of his relatives was going through Dr. Barclay's belongings and found a piece of paper, yellow with age, labeled "An Act of Commitment." It was a written commitment

Barclay had made to God on his sixteenth birthday, when he was a student at Glasgow University. Apparently, he had continued to add his signature every year on his birthday as a way of renewing that commitment. The well-worn paper showed that he had signed the commitment every year from age sixteen to just before he died at eighty-five.

In this act of commitment, Barclay had surrendered his life to God. He had consecrated to God all that he was and all that he had—his mind, his body, his possessions, his time, and his influence over others—to be used for God's glory. He ended his pledge of commitment with these words: "To Thee, O Lord, I leave the management of all events and say without reserve, ... not my will but Thine be done." William Barclay was a true disciple of Jesus Christ.

Like William Barclay's commitment, Mary's loyalty was to God and to doing God's will. Mary's faith was not tentative or conditional; it was total and complete obedience to God, no matter how rough the road might be. Mary's faith was great because she obeyed God's will.

Mary's Faith Was Great Because
She Trusted God's Power

Mary took life one step at a time, one day at a time, trusting God for the future.

Some years ago, there was a captain on a Mississippi riverboat who had held the job for over thirty-five years. One day a passenger said to him, "After all these years of navigating the river, I guess you know where all the rocks and sandbars are."

He answered, "No, but I know where the deep water is!"

That's what Mary said, in effect: I know where the deep water is. I know there are some rocky places out there, but I trust God to bring me through this.

Terry Anderson was serving as the chief Middle East correspondent for the Associated Press when he was kidnapped in Beirut on March 16, 1985. He was held captive until his release on December 4, 1991—almost seven years later. It was an incredibly difficult ordeal, but he came through it all with amazing strength.

Since his release, he has been interviewed a number of times, and his responses are inspirational. Let me share what I consider some of his most powerful comments, which I have collected from various interviews and summarized in my own words.

- First, when he was asked what had enabled him to survive the experience, he answered without hesitation that it was his faith, his companions, and his stubbornness. Trust in God helped to sustain Terry Anderson through his terrible ordeal.
- Second, one reporter reminded him that he had said he didn't hate his captors. When the reporter asked him to help us understand that, he explained that it was really very simple. He was a Christian. The Bible teaches us to forgive, he said, and he didn't hate anyone.
- Third, when he was asked if he ever lost hope, he admitted that he had had some moments of despair. Then he said that, fortunately, one of the first things to fall into his hands after becoming a hostage was a Bible, and that during his captivity he spent a lot of time with the Bible—which is about hope and trust in God. That's what gave him the strength to make it through each day, he said. According to Terry Anderson, the Bible reminded him to do the best he could each day and to trust God for the future.

That's great faith, isn't it? It's the kind of faith Mary had. It's the kind of faith *we* need—faith that enables us to hear God's voice, obey God's will, and trust God's power.

21

2
What Can We Learn from Joseph?

ased on Matthew 1:18-25

A good friend of mine decided to try to make Christmas an especially significant faith experience for his family one year. Three weeks before Christmas, he went out and bought a manger scene to help teach his children the real meaning of the holy season. He purposefully selected one with inexpensive and unbreakable figures so that the children could touch them, pick them up, examine them, and arrange them as they wanted. He then placed the manger scene on the coffee table in the den so that it was easily accessible to the children. It worked like a charm! His daughter, age eight, and son, age five, were so fascinated with the manger scene that they played with it again and again and talked constantly about the little figures in this much-loved, symbolic representation of the first Christmas.

A couple of weeks passed, and then came the "acid test." One day the father sat down with his children and asked them to tell him about the manger scene. With great excitement, they began to point out the characters in the manger scene.

"These are the wise men, and here are their precious gifts," they began. "And these are the camels they rode on. These are the shepherds. And look, they brought some of their sheep with them. And here is the Star of Bethlehem. This is the stable, and these are the barnyard animals. This is the manger, and here are Mary and the Baby Jesus."

"That's great!" said the father, "but didn't you forget somebody? What about him?" Pointing to the figure of Joseph, he asked, "Who is this man standing beside Mary?"

For a moment, there was silence. Both children were deep in thought. Then the five-year-old piped up and said, "Oh, I know. I remember now. That's old 'Joe-what's-his-name'!"

When my friend told me of this interesting and humorous incident, it occurred to me that his children had inadvertently put their finger on a fascinating phenomenon of Christmas: Often we forget about Joseph. There is so much to learn from the great faith of Joseph, and yet over the years we have unconsciously ignored him and pushed him far into the background.

I have to admit my own guilt here. Out of all the Christmas sermons and devotionals and meditations I have given since the beginning of my ministry, I have to confess that I have very rarely mentioned Joseph. Over the years, I have preached many sermons on the Christ Child—and rightly so, for he is, of course, the main message of Christmas. I also have preached about the faith of Mary, the shepherds, the wise men, the star, the manger, the stable, the angels, and even the innkeeper. But through the years I somehow have all but ignored the faith of Joseph, mentioning him only in passing. Joseph is, indeed, the forgotten man of Christmas!

Haunted and intrigued by this realization, I set out to do a little research on the character of Joseph. As I searched for the real Joseph, I was amazed by what I found. In addition to being inspired by the courageous faith of this man, I also discovered that too little attention has been given to Joseph's part in the Gospel story. I came to see that his faith, sensitivity, kindness, compassion, and obedience to the will of God had a greater impact on Christian thought and life than I had ever realized. We owe so much to father Joseph, and we can learn so much from his faith.

Remember his story with me. Joseph was a carpenter of Nazareth when he came to have a tremendously difficult problem. He was jolted by the news that his fiancée, Mary, was expecting a child—before he knew her intimately as a wife. Joseph was crushed, of course; but he loved Mary and did not want to hurt or ridicule or embarrass her.

He agonized over how to handle this difficult situation. As he grappled with his problem, he turned to God—wanting so much to do God's will—and God spoke to him in a dramatic way, saying in effect: "Joseph, don't be afraid. Go ahead and take Mary for your wife. Your love for each other is unique and special. The Spirit is with her, bringing a new life. The child is of God. It is God's will that she will bear a son, and you shall call his name Jesus, for he will save people from their sins."

Joseph obediently did what God told him to do. He took Mary as his wife, and when she bore a son, he named him Jesus. A short time later, Joseph protected his family by taking them to Egypt to escape the wrath of Herod, the King of Judah, who was so threatened by the talk of a newborn king that he wanted to kill the child. Later still, after Herod died, Joseph brought his family back home to Nazareth and took up his carpentry work there.

What else do we know about Joseph? We know from the Scriptures that he came with his family each year to Jerusalem to attend the Feast of Passover. Other than these things, we know little about Joseph. The Gospel writers do not mention him after Jesus began his ministry. At the crucifixion, Jesus asked the disciple John to care for his mother, Mary, suggesting that she was a widow at the time.

Although we don't know a lot about Joseph, what we do know is impressive. In him we see some truly great qualities that challenge us to deeper faith, obedience, and love. Let us explore a few of these qualities and the lessons we can learn from the faith of Joseph. His bigness of spirit challenges us to become better people and better children of God.

Joseph Was Big Enough to Listen

When he first found out that Mary was expecting, Joseph had a problem, a real dilemma. The Scriptures say that "he considered this" (Matthew 1:20 RSV). It sounds so simple and so easy and so quick, but what the Gospel writer was actually saying was that he agonized, he studied, he grappled, he deliberated, he wrestled, he grieved, he wrangled, he struggled, he prayed, and he listened. He listened to Mary, and he listened to God; and the Spirit of God broke through!

What do *you* do when you have a difficult problem? Do you react or lash out or run away or feel sorry for yourself? Or do you, like Joseph, take some time to listen—to other people and to God?

I once read about a politician who made a powerful, rousing speech to some prospective voters. When he finished, he asked with pleading, dramatic flair: "Won't you go to the polls on Tuesday and vote for me?" Just then a heckler in the audience jumped to his feet and yelled: "I wouldn't vote for you if you were St. Peter!" Quick as a flash, the politician rose to the occasion and answered, "If I were St. Peter, you wouldn't be in my district!"

I wish I were as quick as that in response to my problems, but often I go down a lot of painful roads seeking answers that are sometimes awfully hard to come by. I have to do a lot of listening. Joseph listened out of wisdom; I listen out of necessity! When I have a problem, I need all the help I can get. Most of us do.

Sooner or later, every one of us comes up against the rough side of life, and we have to face big problems. Dr. J. A. Hadfield, noted British psychologist, commented on this when he said, "When people run up against life and find it too much for them, one swears, one gets a headache, one gets drunk and one prays" (*Psychology and Morals*, Robert Hadfield Co., 1935; page 55).

When life gets hard, what do *you* do? Do you give up? Do you swear? Do you lash out in hostility? Do you try to find someone to blame? Do you give in to bitterness? Do you run away? Do you hide behind some illness? Do you drug yourself? Or do you pray? Do you consider the problem prayerfully and then listen for God? That's what Joseph did, and it worked.

What a great lesson to learn from Joseph: the art of listening! Maybe this is why Jesus went often into the wilderness alone to do some praying and listening. Perhaps he learned from father Joseph how to listen for God's will.

Joseph was big enough to listen. What a wonderful quality!

Joseph Was Big Enough to Obey

Even when it was hard to do, Joseph listened and heard God's command. Then he had the courage to act, to obey, to do God's will.

When I think of obedience to God, so many dramatic images flood into my mind.

- There is Job, facing pain and disaster, saying, "Though he slay me, yet will I trust in him!" (Job 13:15 KJV).
- There is Moses, confronting the awesome power of the Pharaoh and saying, "Let my people go!" (Exodus 5:1).
- There is the missionary Elisabeth Eliot, who went back to work with the Auca Indians after they had brutally murdered her closest loved ones. She is reported to have said that she was certain of one thing: that she must obey God.

- There is George Frideric Handel. Every time I hear the "Hallelujah!" chorus, I think of how it almost didn't get written. Handel was beset with great troubles. His health and his fortune had reached the lowest ebb. His right side had become paralyzed, and all his money was gone. His creditors seized him and threatened him with imprisonment. For a brief time, he was tempted to quit, to give up the fight; but then, like Joseph, his obedience to God welled up within him, and he rebounded to compose his greatest work, the epic *Messiah*, the second part of which ends majestically with the powerful "Hallelujah!" chorus.
- The best example of obedience is Jesus in the Garden of Gethsemane. In the shadow of a dark, looming, painful cross, he prayed, "Not my will, Father, but your will be done!" (Matthew 26:42, author's paraphrase).

If love was the key quality in Jesus' life and character, then obedience ran a close second. We are touched by his compassion and mercy and kindness, but at the center of his life was a tremendous, unswerving obedience to God's will.

It is often said, "Like Father, like son." Joseph, too, is the picture of obedience. Despite shame, uncertainty, and fear, Joseph had the courage to do what God asked him to do. Joseph was big enough to obey. What a wonderful quality!

Joseph Was Big Enough to Honor God By the Way He Lived

I think it's safe to say that much of what Jesus learned, he learned from Joseph. Joseph must have been a wonderful father, because when Jesus grew up he called God "Father," and that was a good image in his mind. When Jesus wanted to help us understand God, he said that God is like an understanding father. Jesus felt Joseph's love; he saw his grace and compassion, his mercy and kindness; he experienced his strong "watchcare." And Jesus must have said: "God is like that! God is like a loving parent! He cares for his children like father Joseph cares for me!"

A few Christmases ago, a man showed up at the church I was serving, looking for assistance. I gave him some food, some shoes, a coat, a suitcase, some medicine, and a bus ticket to Florida. Shortly after he left, I realized that even while I was making the arrangements to help him, he had stolen a cut glass paperweight from my desk. The paperweight was not that valuable, but it was special to me because it had been a gift from some cherished friends.

I felt hurt, abused, and violated! I found myself wondering why it bothered me so much. Then I realized that it was because I felt dehumanized—rejected as a person. I thought that if he really knew me as a person, he wouldn't have stolen from me. I felt like a pigeon, an object, a thing used and discarded—not a person.

But then I realized something very significant: The good news of our faith is that God sees all of us as persons! Even better, God wants to claim all of us as his children! That's what Jesus taught us—perhaps in large part because of the example of his own father, Joseph.

Of course, not all of us have loving parents. Neither can all of us be model parents. But Joseph teaches us that despite the difficulties we may face, we can become better persons and better children of God by listening to God's voice, obeying God's will, and honoring God by the way we live. Like Joseph, we can exemplify those genuinely godlike qualities that lead to deeper faith, obedience, and love.

3

What Can We Learn from an Innkeeper?

ased on Luke 2:1-7

Do you remember the 1960s? Those were hard, difficult years filled with protests and demonstrations. Let me tell you about one very unusual demonstration that took place during that period of time.

The year was 1965. It was Christmas Eve. An innkeeper at one of the hotels in town had had a busy day. It was late, and he was at the main desk, alone. Although the inn was full of Christmas travelers, he had sent most of the workers home to be with their families for Christmas Eve. The lobby was relatively quiet now.

As he was doing some paperwork at the front desk, he heard a noise and looked up. He couldn't believe his eyes. Walking through the lobby door on this Christmas Eve was a young man dressed in a biblical costume. Actually, it was an old, tattered bathrobe. The young man was pulling a donkey. Riding on the donkey was a young woman who looked to be quite expectant.

As they approached the desk, the young man announced loudly for all to hear: "My name is Joseph, and this is Mary. As you can see, she is about to have a baby. We need a room for the night."

Before I tell you the rest of the story, let me share with you what was really happening on that Christmas Eve in 1965. The young man's name was not Joseph, and the young woman was not Mary. And she was not really expecting a baby. This true incident was designed to be a kind of political demonstration against the commercialization of Christmas. Since there had been a "no vacancy" sign up for several hours, this modern-day Mary and Joseph fully expected to be turned away. In fact, they wanted to be turned away. They were certain that they would be told there was "no room in the inn" for them. Their plan was to go to the media with the story of their rejection.

But the innkeeper dealt the demonstrators a big surprise that night. He rushed around the desk and welcomed them warmly and graciously: "Mary and Joseph, how great it is to have you with us! You honor us by coming here tonight. What a privilege to have you under our roof! It's true that all our regular rooms are taken, but we would be so pleased if you would occupy the bridal suite. And, of course, since it's Christmas Eve, there will be no charge. You will be our special guests of honor!"

That's what I call rising to the occasion! That innkeeper proved to be very wise, didn't he? He knew the Christmas story, and he had something of the spirit of Christmas within him. He also was extremely shrewd because he knew how harshly history can deal with an unsuspecting innkeeper.

That creative innkeeper has haunted me ever since I first read of the incident many years ago. He jolted my conscience and made me look in a fresh, new way at the innkeeper in the original Christmas story. He smashed the windowpanes of my stereotyped image of the innkeeper and let new winds blow into my mind. He enabled me to see the innkeeper from a different perspective, which sent me scrambling for my Bible and resource books in search of a new understanding of the original innkeeper, who has become such a prominent figure in our Christmas pageants.

When we look at the innkeeper with an open mind, important and universal truths about life stand up and stare us in the face. Let us explore some of the significant and helpful lessons that we can learn from him.

The Innkeeper Teaches Us a Lesson About Prejudice

The innkeeper teaches us about the danger of judging people and events without having all the facts, and of letting our imaginations run wild. When we judge other people or assess events without knowing the whole truth, the results can be unfair, dangerous, damaging, and destructive.

I suspect that we have treated the innkeeper unfairly. History has dealt with him harshly. We have sternly written him off as a bad character, when the truth is that we know virtually nothing about him. How fascinated we have been with this innkeeper. He has captured the imagination of poets and playwrights, preachers and songwriters, artists, and storytellers. We have pictured him as a harsh, irritable, insensitive character who was too caught up in his own self-centered world to be concerned about the problems of others; who was too cold and calculating to be bothered even by a young couple who were obviously expecting a baby at any moment. We have pictured him as arrogant and impatient, with a loud, booming voice and big, burly arms, pushing the young couple out into the cold street with harsh words: "Get out! We're full up. No room here. I can't be bothered with you and your problems. I have problems enough of my own!"

It fascinates me that we have pictured him so vividly. In fact, it's rather amazing, because he is not even mentioned in any of the biblical accounts of the Christmas story! All of these negative, demeaning characteristics have been attached to the innkeeper because of an implication in one portion of one verse of scripture in Luke's Gospel: "no room...in the inn" (2:7 KJV). The entire verse reads: "And she brought forth her firstborn son, and wrapped him in swaddling clothes, and laid him in a manger; because there was no room for them in the inn" (KJV). That's all it says: no room in the inn. With those five words we have performed a character assassination on an innkeeper, on a man, on a person, on a child of God we know nothing about.

There's a valuable lesson here that we all need to learn, and it is this: It is destructive to judge people and events when we don't really know the situation or circumstances or facts. We should never let our imaginations run wild. When we judge others without the whole truth, we can cause a lot of confusion and heartache.

There's a story about two men who met on the street. One said to the other, "Hey, I know you. You're the man from the state of Maine who made one million dollars in growing potatoes."

"Yes," the second man replied, "but your facts are a little confused. It isn't Maine; it's Georgia. It isn't potatoes; it's cotton. It isn't *made* one million dollars; it's *lost* one million dollars. And it isn't me; it's my brother! Other than that, you got it just right!"

We often get confused and get our facts mixed up!

A few years ago, the *London Daily Telegraph* carried a letter sent by an eleven-year-old boy to his mother while he was on vacation in Switzerland. Here's what he wrote:

Dear Mom,
    Yesterday the instructor took eight of us to the slopes to teach us to ski. I was not very good at it, so I broke a leg. Thank goodness it wasn't mine!
    Love, Billy

From that information, we are not sure what happened on the ski slopes of Switzerland—or how to assess it. This is an oft-repeated dimension of life. It is harmful to judge when we are confused about the facts—or before all the facts are in.

That's the first lesson we can learn from the innkeeper: the danger of prejudice. It's destructive and hurtful to judge people or to look down our noses at them when we don't have all the facts—when we don't know the whole truth. We need to beware of prejudice.

The Innkeeper Teaches Us a Lesson About Choices

Often our choices are not so much between right and wrong or good and bad as they are between the lesser of two bad things. The innkeeper really didn't have a good choice that night. The sleepy little town of Bethlehem suddenly was packed with visitors. Caesar had sent out the order that the people be enrolled for tax purposes. Everyone had to return to his or her hometown for the census. Bethlehem was bursting at the seams.

In those days, hotels operated on a first-come, first-served basis, and every available room was taken. When Joseph and Mary came to his door that night, the innkeeper had to make a decision. Would he send away those who already were settled in to make room for the latecomers? It was not an easy choice to make. What would you have done if you had been in his place?

Biblical commentator William Barclay suggests that the innkeeper may have been the only friend Mary and Joseph had that night in Bethlehem. Tradition suggests that he sent them to a cave near the inn to spend the night. There were some good reasons for that decision.

Hotels in those days were hardly luxurious. Most of them were two-story buildings. The upper floor was used for the guests—without much privacy—and the first floor was set aside for the animals upon which the people traveled. Hotels were cold, smelly places; and that night they were crowded and noisy—hardly a place for the birth of a baby.

But Bethlehem afforded another possibility. Built on a ridge of limestone, the town had numerous caves. Some of these caves were used as stables. They were not much better for an expectant mother, but at least there was warmth and quiet and some privacy. If this is what happened on that night long ago, then our whole image of the innkeeper changes dramatically. We view him not with contempt, but with kindness. Any decision he could have made would have been imperfect. He could only choose the lesser of evils that night, and he may well have made a wise, loving choice.

The real key in whatever we choose and in whatever we do is our attitude. Jesus talked frequently about the importance of our attitudes and motivations. He was supremely interested in them.

Think about the innkeeper. If, on the one hand, he said to Mary and Joseph, "Get out of here. I'm full up. I don't have time to be bothered with the likes of you," then that's one thing. On the other hand, if he said to Mary and Joseph, "Look, my friends, all my spaces here in the hotel are taken, but I know a place . . . ," then that's a different story. The difference is in the attitude.

The innkeeper teaches us that we must prayerfully make the best choices we can based on the best information we have—*with a loving, compassionate attitude*—and then go forward, trusting God to bring it out right.

The Innkeeper Teaches Us a Lesson About God

The innkeeper's story underscores one of the greatest truths and promises of the scriptures and of our faith: namely, that God can turn defeats into victories. God can take bad things and redeem them and make them good.

You see, there were other hands at work that night in Bethlehem. God took the innkeeper's decision and let Jesus, God's Son, be born in a stable. God then took the stable and hallowed it, so that it has become one of the most important and beautiful symbols in all the world. The lowliness of Christ's birth became an asset in the hands of God—not a liability. God takes our actions and judgments and redeems them and makes good come from them. A little more than thirty years later, God did the same thing with a cross.

In his book *Faith, Hope, and Hilarity*, Dick Van Dyke tells about a child who was called away from watching the six o'clock news on television to say the blessing at the evening meal. The child, with his mind still on the calamities of the newscast, said the blessing and then added a personal note: "Dear God, please take care of Mommy and Daddy and my little sister and Gramma and all the people in the world— and please, God, take good care of yourself because if anything happens to you, we are all sunk" (Doubleday, 1970).

There is something of my own faith in that prayer. I realize that I have neither the wisdom nor the intelligence to always make the right decisions. Sometimes my guesses may be good; at other times—too many times—they are wrong. But, you know, I'm glad God has not left us alone. God is with us. So, in spite of our blunders and mistakes and poor judgments and tough choices and clay feet, God carries on his work. God works through us, sometimes despite our weaknesses. That's the good news of Christmas: God is with us and is working for us.

4
What Can We Learn from the Christ Child?

ased on Luke 2:8-14

A few years ago, I had the privilege of touring the Holy Land. It was a magnificent experience. What a thrill it was to see the Jordan River, the Sea of Galilee, the Mount of Olives, the Mount of Transfiguration, the ancient market-place, the Upper Room, the Garden of Gethsemane, the Garden of Resurrection, the village of Jericho, and the holy city of Jerusalem. Just being in those historic and sacred places was wonderfully mind-boggling to me. As we traveled back to our hotel at the end of each day, tired but exhilarated, I found myself subconsciously humming "I Walked Today Where Jesus Walked" and sensing something of what the songwriter must have felt when he first penned those words.

Then early one morning we started toward Bethlehem. Bethlehem—we were actually going to that sacred place where the Christ Child was born. I couldn't wait. Even though it was January, I was ready for some Christmas in

Bethlehem. As the tour bus slowed to enter the city, I casually glanced out the window. I couldn't believe my eyes. There on the Bethlehem hillside were some shepherds keeping watch over their flocks. It looked like a perfect scenario for a Christmas card. I was touched and inspired by the simple, serene splendor of that sight.

When we finally arrived in the city, it was anything but serene splendor! It was total chaos—loud music, gaudy signs, crass commercialism, merchants shouting and hawking their souvenirs as if there were no tomorrow, people milling and pushing and shoving, poor children everywhere begging for "one American dollar," and our tour director warning us to watch out for pickpockets.

"Wait a minute!" I wanted to scream. "This is Bethlehem, not Bourbon Street! This is Bethlehem, not Times Square!" It was indeed Bethlehem, but it seemed more like bedlam. I wanted Christmas, but it felt like confusion! My heart sank. I felt let down, disappointed, disillusioned.

As we walked into the Church of the Nativity and came to the spot built to honor Christ's birth, I was amazed to see that the same carnival-like atmosphere prevailed there too. Even there in the chapel it was loud, boisterous, commercial, and chaotic—with hucksters selling trinkets, T-shirts, pictures, and postcards. My spirit sagged even more. I wanted Bethlehem, but it was all bedlam.

But then, something happened to change everything. A little girl who looked to be six or seven years old was standing in the chapel with her mother. Her mother was explaining that this was the place where Jesus was born on the first Christmas. Suddenly, in the midst of all the hucksters and merchants, the sightseers and tourists, that little girl did a beautiful thing. She dropped to her knees, bowed her head, and said, "Thank you, God, for sending Jesus! Amen."

As I heard the simple, sincere prayer of that little girl, suddenly it was Christmas in my heart! Once again, Christmas had come through a little child. Bedlam had become Bethlehem.

It was a touching moment, and it made me realize something that we all need to remember: Christmas happens right in the midst of our confusion. We don't have to choose between Bethlehem and bedlam. They go together. They always have. That's the good news, isn't it? God breaks into our confusion—into the bedlam—and makes himself known!

Christmas and confusion: Weren't they intimately related at the first Christmas when Jesus was born? Remember the bedlam in Bethlehem that night. Talk about chaos! Talk about confusion! Just think of it: a crowded inn, a stable, a census, long lines, political intrigue, soldiers marching in the streets, a busy city, people pushing and shoving, people worrying about how to make ends meet. In that confusion, Christmas happened. In that bedlam, Christmas broke through. In that busy, hectic uproar, it happened; and those with eyes and ears and hearts of faith saw it, heard it, and felt it! That's the way it always works.

This, you see, is the good news of Christmas: God meets us where we are! God breaks into our uproar, our busyness, our hectic pace, our darkness and makes himself known as the King of kings, as the Light of the world, and as the gracious Lord who understands and forgives and cares and saves. Despite all the confusion, the spirit of Christmas—the real meaning of Christmas—breaks through the fog, the bedlam, and clears things up. Let's consider this more carefully by looking together at what we can learn from the Christ Child.

The Christ Child Teaches Us What God Is Like

Christmas clears up our confusion about God. Christmas shows us what God is like. It gives us a new picture, and what this picture reveals is "good news," "glad tidings."

A seven-year-old boy had been playing outside. His mother called him in for dinner. The little boy ran in, jumped into his chair, and grabbed his fork, ready to eat.

"Wait, Tommy," said his mom, "you have germs on your

hands. Go wash up before we eat." Tommy scrambled down, ran and washed his hands, came back, climbed up into his chair, grabbed his fork, and started to eat.

Again his mother stopped him. "Wait, Tommy," she said, "we must say the blessing before we eat. We want to thank God for our food."

Little Tommy put down his fork, mournfully shook his head, and muttered wearily, "Germs and God, germs and God. That's all I ever hear around here, and I ain't never seen neither one of them!"

We can sympathize with Tommy's predicament. Yet Christmas does give us some help, because Christmas gives God a face. Christmas shows us who God is and what God is like.

In his commentary *The Gospel of Matthew*, William Barclay put it like this:

> Jesus is the one person who can tell us what God is like, and what God means us to be. In Jesus alone we see what God is like, and we see what man ought to be like. Before Jesus came men had only vague and shadowy, and often quite wrong, ideas about God; they could only at best guess and grope; but Jesus could say, "He that hath seen Me hath seen the Father" (John 14:9). In Jesus we see the love, the compassion, the mercy, the seeking heart, the purity of God as nowhere else in all this world. With the coming of Jesus the time of guessing is gone, and the time of certainty is come....Jesus came to tell us the truth about God and the truth about ourselves.
>
> (Westminster Press, 1956, vol. I; page 11)

This is the "good news" of Christmas. Jesus shows us what God is like, and the word is *love*. God is not an angry judge who must be appeased. God is not a powermonger, demanding his "pound of flesh." God is like a loving parent, who cares and understands, who is concerned about the welfare of his or her children.

It is interesting to note how often Jesus said "Fear not," "Don't be afraid," or "Fret no more." It is also interesting to note in Luke's Gospel, the first thing the angel said to the shepherds: "Do not be afraid; for see—I am bringing you good news" (2:10). This is the most significant gift of Christmas! God gives us a new understanding of what God is like, a new experience of God's compassion and tenderness, a new relationship with God—built not of fear, but of love. You see, Christmas breaks into the wild confusion and bedlam, and the Christ Child reminds us that God is a loving parent. That's the good news of Christmas, and that's what keeps us going.

The Christ Child Teaches Us That We Are Family

Christmas clears up our confusion about how to relate to other people. Christmas gives us new respect and regard for others. Christmas breaks through the fog and shows us that people are more important than things, that people are not pawns to be used and manipulated but persons to be loved and appreciated. Christmas reminds us that we are family.

In a "Peanuts" comic strip, Charlie Brown and Linus are watching television. Snoopy is standing on top of the TV set, his ears sticking up in a V shape. He is serving as the antennae. Then Charlie Brown says to Linus, "I don't understand it either. All I know is that he gives us a better picture!"

The same thing could be said about Christmas, couldn't it? I don't understand everything about the coming of the Christ Child. All I know is that he gives us a better picture. He sharpens the image. He clears up the confusion and shows us not only what God is like, but also what God wants us to be like. Christmas shows us dramatically that the best way to show our love for God is to love God's children.

Some years ago, a letter came to our home that moved me as much as any letter I have ever read. It was from a friend named Wanda. Wanda had invited me to speak at a special

Christmas program at her church early in December. Because of the hectic pace of the Christmas rush, I really didn't think I should go; but because of my appreciation for Wanda, I accepted and went.

Two days after I spoke at her church, the letter came. It was from Wanda. But it was not addressed to me! It was addressed to our children, Jodi and Jeff. They were six and nine at the time. Here is part of the letter.

Dear Jodi & Jeff,

> I know most of the mail that comes to your house goes to your mom and dad, so I wanted to write to you. I am writing to thank you for sharing your dad with our community. You are so nice to share him with others, and I want you to know that I appreciate it.
> Love, Wanda

When the children let me see the letter, my eyes filled with tears. I was so touched by her thoughtfulness—much more than I would have been had the letter been written to me. She wrote to my children, and that touched me!

Then it broke through to me: That's what Christmas is all about. Love for the children is the best way to show love for the Father! If you want to express your love and appreciation to God, the best way to do it is to love God's children.

This is what the prophets meant when they said that God doesn't care about burnt offerings or sacrifices or lavish prayers. What God really wants is for us to be merciful, kind, forgiving, thoughtful, and loving toward one another. That's why Christ came—to show us how to care for others, to remind us that we are family. That's the good news of Christmas, and that's what keeps us going.

The Christ Child Teaches Us How to Love

Christmas clears up our confusion about what love is. A few years ago, noted minister and author Hoover Rupert told about a beautiful incident that took place at the Mohawk Central School in New York state. The principal of that school was concerned that some of the children were from impoverished families and would have no Christmas gifts. He set up a Santa's Helpers Fund and encouraged students to contribute, if they were able, so that gifts might be bought for the underprivileged children in the area.

One thirteen-year-old boy was touched by the idea. He scrimped and saved for weeks so he could help some poor child to have Christmas gifts that year. He managed to raise fifteen cents. On the day the contributions were to be received, which was the last day before Christmas vacation, there was a terrible blizzard, and school was canceled. With snow and ice everywhere, no buses were running.

Convinced that there would be someone at the school to receive his money, this thirteen-year-old boy walked through the blizzard to the school and placed his fifteen cents into the hands of the principal. As the boy turned to go back out into the blizzard and head home, the principal had to swallow hard and blink back the tears, because he knew that this boy's name was on the list of underprivileged children who were to receive gifts from the Santa's Helpers Fund.

That boy knew what love is. He had within him the true spirit of Christmas: unselfish, sacrificial love. That's the good news of Christmas, and that's what keeps us going.

It's so easy to give in to the temptation to complain about the bedlam of Christmas. It's so easy to complain about the confusion and commercialism and say, "Oh, I can't get into the spirit of Christmas anymore. They have ruined it." One writer called this a kind of "Christianized humbugging." Don't give in to that attitude, because come what may, Christmas is going to happen! Christmas is going to happen right in the middle of all the confusion and chaos. I hope and pray that you will be ready to see it, hear it, feel it, and share it this year—as never before!

REFLECTION

Nell W. Mohney

*et your light so shine before [others],
that they may see your good works, and glorify
your Father which is in heaven.*
—Matthew 5:16 KJV

"The Visited Planet," by J. B. Phillips, tells of a veteran angel showing a new angel around the universe. After showing off the brilliant lights, the guide pointed out a little speck next to a beautiful star. "That star is the sun, and the speck is the earth."

The new angel asked, "What's so special about the speck?"

The veteran angel replied: "That is the visited planet. The Father himself became one of them and chose them to be his own. He gave his life on a cross for them."

"Then why is the earth so dark?" asked the new angel.

"Because many people haven't decided to accept God's choice. They haven't decided whether to live in light or darkness."

PART TWO

The Cradle and the Star

Reginald Mallett

INTRODUCTION

The Cradle

"What can we use for a crib?" It was the midwife who asked the question. She had summoned me to a poor home in a remote area hoping that I could succeed where she had failed. She had tried to persuade a young woman who was in early labor to go to the hospital. I also failed. The expectant mother was adamant in her refusal. She had vowed that her first baby would be born at home, and our united entreaties could not shake her resolve.

It was mid-December, and events had taken the couple by surprise. The baby was arriving three weeks early. As a newly qualified doctor, I was profoundly grateful for the presence of such a wise and experienced midwife. Thankfully, the delivery went well. Then, as the mother held her newborn daughter, we realized that no provision had been made for a cradle. The midwife, a very practical woman, went to her car and returned with a strong cardboard carton. With some minor modifications and suitably lined, it sufficed.

As I left two happy and thankful parents and drove home through streets lined with shops made bright with festive Christmas lights, I thought of the child in her improvised cradle. It was not the first time that a humble object had been adapted for such a noble use. Once, a manger, an animal feeding trough, served a similar purpose. A manger, just pieces of wood no doubt crudely joined together, became the cradle for the Savior of the world. Hymn-writer Charles Wesley captures the wonder of it in his lines:

> Stand amazed ye heavens at this!
> See the Lord of earth and skies;
> Humbled to the dust he is
> And in a manger lies.

At Bethlehem we see the humanity of God in coming as a helpless baby and relying upon an earthly mother for warmth and food. As we journey toward Christmas and look forward to the hope of the ages being fulfilled in Christ, we are reminded that when God stepped onto the stage of recorded history, very ordinary instruments were used. God chose a poor young couple, a rustic animal shelter, and an improvised cradle. The manger has become a symbol of the God who fully shares our helplessness and humanity.

But Also a Star!

The star is the symbol of the other part of the story. It reminds us that Christmas is not just about a simple, devout couple and a baby, but also about God and a love that reaches out to humanity. Two great theological words grasp hands in this holy season. The first is *immanence*—God here with us, represented by the manger, a humble cradle. The second is *transcendence*—God beyond us, altogether other, eternal, and all-powerful, represented by the star.

With the arrival of the Advent season, our spirits begin to rise. Cheerful, festive decorations appear in the stores and the streets. Sprigs of holly, frosted windows, candles, and colored lights work their Christmas magic. Memories of childhood return. For Christians, however, this time of the year has much deeper significance. For many whose hearts ache with inexpressible fears and hurts, this wonderful season offers a comfort that cannot be found in any gaily wrapped present, no matter how generous or how kindly meant. Advent offers *hope*. The hope that God is at work in the world. The hope that human sinfulness will not have the final word. The hope that there is a road that stretches from the cradle to the star along which we ordinary folk may travel to the heart of God.

In his book *Principalities and Powers* (Epworth Press, 1952; page 40), my friend and teacher Professor Gordon Rupp tells of a moving story that emerged during the Nuremberg war crimes trials at the end of World War II. A large number of Jews were being mown down by machine-gun fire across open graves. Among them stood an old man and a little boy. Before they died, the old man bent down and spoke to the boy. What he said will never be known, but as they died, the old Jew raised his right arm and pointed to the sky. In the end that is the story of the people of God, as from the beginning they have pointed beyond history to the coming righteousness of God. The Christian church has entered into this heritage. It too, like the spires of its churches, points upward, beyond history to the eternal, from the cradle to the star. The Advent hope is that just as God intervened in history in the baby of the manger, so God's purposes will ultimately be fulfilled in spite of human waywardness and sin. Throughout the season the hope rings out that one day heaven will sing: "The kingdoms of this world are become the kingdoms of our Lord, and of his Christ; and he shall reign for ever and ever" (Revelation 11:15 KJV).

So before we plunge into the joyful preparations for Christmas, before we are overwhelmed by the shopping, the writing of cards, the planning of parties and special services in church, let us pause and reflect on this wonder. Let us journey toward Christmas thrilled by the immanence and the transcendence of God. Thrilled that God holds in one hand the cradle and in the other the star.

5

The Friend of God

based on James 2:23

A woman lay critically ill in the hospital. Her husband, a rough diamond, was a manual worker whom higher education has passed by. He did not find it easy to express himself as I emerged from her hospital room and sat down to talk with him. Gently, I coaxed the conversation along. His three grown children stood by as I tried to describe her condition in nonmedical terms. I concluded by saying that I was sure she had a fighting chance. Tears of hope and relief welled up in his eyes, and then almost immediately he became embarrassed by what he thought was a display of weakness; and he apologized for his tears. I hastened to reassure him. "Don't be ashamed of your emotions," I said. "It is natural for a man to feel so deeply about his wife." He then took my hand in his and in a soft voice almost whispered what at first sounded strange. "She is more than that, doctor," he said. "She is my one true friend."

His words echoed in my mind as I wandered down the

hospital corridor after leaving him. No poet could more eloquently have expressed what this man felt: "My one true friend." It was an unusual way of expressing a marriage relationship. It spoke of a bonding that, born perhaps in romance, had been tempered by the experiences of delight and disappointment that he and his wife had shared as they reared their growing family on very limited means. Over the years something precious had been forged between them, a deep, loving companionship that he movingly described by saying, "She is my one true friend."

Christmas is a season of hope. The longings of the ages were to be fulfilled in the coming of the Christ Child. But the story of God's redemption did not begin in Roman occupied Bethlehem. It is important to set the Advent hope in its historical context, for it began centuries earlier in the tents of a man who had set out on a journey of faith. That man, Abraham, is regarded by three of the world's great religions as a founding father. He is inseparably bound up with the story of God's people.

Abraham alone in the Hebrew Scriptures is singled out from the distinguished gallery of great men and women of faith who prepared the way for the coming of the Messiah, and he is given a special title. Of all the accolades and laurel wreaths, of all the compliments and honors bestowed on anyone who belonged to the community of faith, none was greater than that given to Abraham. His is the unique honor of being called "the friend of God." Others may have been honored by the title "Servant of God," but no other was called "God's friend."

What was so special about this man who before the coming of the Christ Child should be given so lofty a title? Certainly it did not lie in his saintly character. It may come as a surprise to discover that he was vulnerable and frail. Of course, he was a good man, but the Bible makes no attempt to hide the flaws both in his character and in his somewhat dysfunctional family. And yet with all his faults, he played a pivotal part in establishing the nation that would serve as the crucible in which God would prepare the right conditions for the coming of Jesus. As we think of the hope that was to be embodied in a child lying in a crude cradle, heralded by a song of angels and signaled by a star, it will help us prepare for Christmas to travel back across the centuries and learn the secret of one who was called "the friend of God."

Abraham Became God's Friend by Obeying God's Call

I was recently asked to introduce Dr. Mathan, the director of the Christian Medical College and Hospital in Vellore, India, to a lunchtime audience. The meeting was organized by the local branch of "The Friends of Vellore."

It was an unforgettable experience. A distinguished gastroenterologist, Dr. Mathan directs what is the largest medical center on the Indian subcontinent. The work is supported by forty-six denominations in ten countries, and his responsibilities take him around the world. We were overwhelmed by this gracious, gentle man who almost succeeded in hiding his tremendous scholarship and enormous achievements with his self-effacing modesty.

When he began to speak he did not start with himself or his work. Instead he held us enthralled by relating the story of the call of Ida Skudder, the remarkable woman who began the vast enterprise which he now leads.

It was in 1890 that eighteen-year-old Ida was summoned to India by her father, a missionary doctor, because her mother was ill. She left the United States determined that the visit would be brief. It was her firm resolve, just as soon as her mother had recovered, to return to complete her college education and enjoy the free life of a young woman in a land of opportunity. Become a missionary like so many in her remarkable family? Certainly not!

One night, out there in India, however, everything changed. Sitting at her desk in her parents' little bungalow, she was disturbed three times by distressed husbands who wanted her to come and assist their young wives who were struggling in difficult childbirth. Custom and caste forbade their accepting the help of her medically qualified father. That would be unthinkable. He was a man! Ida was helpless. Without training she would be more a hindrance than a help. Crestfallen, she had to turn them away and then passed the night in disturbed heart-searching.

Early the next morning she heard the beating of drums in the village and feared the significance of that ominous sound. With a heavy heart she asked the servant to go and make inquiries about the fate of the three women who had been on her mind all night. He returned to tell her that each of them was dead.

Dr. Mathan went on to tell us how that day Ida Skudder was offered a date with destiny. The lives of four young women seemed to reach out and touch one another in the darkness. They never met. They came from different countries. They belonged to different religions; one was a Christian, one a Muslim, and two were Hindus. But the Spirit of God moved over the face of that darkness and planted a hope and a vision in the heart of the eighteen-year-old American girl. In her despair, she heard God calling, and she kept her date with destiny.

Nine years later, graduating in medicine from Cornell Medical College, Dr. Ida, as she became known, returned to Vellore, India, to found a hospital for women and children.

It had not been her original plan to become a missionary. It was not what she had wanted or expected, but she responded in faith. And from that seed of faith a mighty oak has grown. Because she obeyed God, a vast enterprise far exceeding anyone's imagination has come into being. Today it is a 1,700-bed medical center, the leading hospital and medical school in India with graduates working all over the world from its 84 training programs in medical, nursing, and paramedical fields.

In obedience and faith, a young woman obeyed the divine call and became the friend of God. Like Abraham of old, she went out not really knowing where she was going. As a result, the sick are healed, the lame walk, the blind see, and the lepers are cleansed. So identified did this woman become with the people of India that a letter from an American friend that had on the envelope just the words "Dr. Ida—India" was delivered to her doorstep. She became the friend of God and the herald of hope to a subcontinent.

It is not such a great leap of thought from this amazing woman in India to a patriarch living thousands of years earlier. God called Abraham on a journey that had no clear destination. Common sense would have cautioned Abraham against leaving Ur in Chaldea. But he saw the star of God's guiding hand, and he obeyed. "He set out, not knowing where he was going" (Hebrews 11:8) and, as a result, became "the friend of God," giving birth to a hope that one day all would share in that divine friendship.

In the Christmas season we are reminded how centuries later this hope was fulfilled in the coming of the Christ Child. As men and women responded in obedience to the call of Jesus, they heard the words "I do not call you servants any longer. . . . I have called you friends" (John 15:15). Obedience is the doorway through which, this Christmastime, we may enter into a very special relationship with God.

Abraham Became God's Friend by Looking Steadfastly to the Eternal

Some years ago I heard a rather pathetic story of a young couple who had bought an old house just outside an English city. They were desperately short of money, so they tried to cut down on the expenses by doing the legal work themselves. At first they were ignorant of the fact that a new highway was planned, which would come straight through their house. When they eventually found out, they thought that by making the old house sufficiently presentable they would be able to persuade the authorities to divert the new road in order to spare their home. They spent more than a year working on it, investing every spare moment of their time and every penny they possessed to renovate the old property. Through their efforts they accomplished wonders. They patched up the cracked walls and covered them with attractive wallpaper. Outdated, dilapidated cupboards were replaced with modern ones. They had a new front door and new window frames fitted. Out went the old shabby kitchen cabinets and in came handsome new ones. They even had an electrician friend come and renew the electrical wiring. The house began to look quite smart, and they felt proud of their achievements. The couple were confident they were there to stay.

And then it happened. One day a letter arrived telling them that the date for demolition had been set and giving them a month's notice to vacate the property. They were shattered. They thought of all the time, energy, and expense they had put into that old house. So much of themselves had been invested in a building destined to be bulldozed to the ground. They had lost sight of the fact that they were living under an eviction order.

It is a common folly. We easily forget that we are only temporary tenants of the earthly house God has lent us. Our tenure is very limited, and we are foolish if we overlook the wider dimension of eternity. Abraham made no such mistake. The tents he lived in were a continual reminder that he was only traveling through. He never forgot that he was only a temporary resident. "For he looked forward to the city that has foundations, whose architect and builder is God" (Hebrews 11:10).

The message of Christmas rings out: Look up! See how the God who found in Abraham a friend reached out through the child of Bethlehem to an estranged humanity. "In Christ God was reconciling the world to himself" (2 Corinthians 5:19).

The wonder of it: Because of the Savior's coming, ordinary men and women might become the friends of God! But there is more. Christmas not only points back in time to the marvelous events that happened two thousand years ago. It also points forward, reminding us of the thrilling hope that one day all things will be gloriously summed up in Christ. Happy, therefore, are they who fix their eyes, not on the things that are destined to pass away, but on the things that last forever. Happy, because they thus become the friends of God.

Abraham Became God's Friend by Holding Nothing Back from God

Few stories in the Bible so grip the imagination as that in which Abraham is prepared to offer up Isaac to God. It is impossible to understand the patriarch's relationship with God without examining this story carefully.

Here is a picture in two parts. In the first, Abraham, accompanied by his happy, carefree son, is painfully making his way to the top of a hill with anguish in his heart. The journey begun two days earlier is now reaching its completion. The elderly father and his young son have left the two servants with the donkey down in the valley, and the two of them climb together. As they did so, turmoil must have been boiling in the heart of the old man. Why had he felt an inner compulsion to do something utterly repulsive to all his natural feelings? Why was he so sure that God wanted him to destroy everything that had been so carefully built up? How could a God of mercy want him to do something so merciless?

But he could not escape it. The conviction had grown and grown until it had become an obsession. He must have tossed in his tent, unable to sleep as he struggled with it. We can imagine him standing beneath the open heavens, asking the question "Why?" The insistent prodding would not, however, go away; God seemed to want what was most precious in his life. Nothing was to be held back. And for Abraham, accustomed to a culture of sacrifice, this could mean only one thing.

And so the old man toils up the hill with Isaac, who carries the wood on his back for his father's sacrifice. As they near the brow of the hill, the boy voices his bewilderment. "The fire and wood are here, but where is the lamb for a burnt offering?" The father looks at him with eyes full of pain, and love. "God himself will provide the lamb for a burnt offering, my son" (Genesis 22:7-8). What questions Abraham must have been asking himself at that moment. *Is this where the dream ends? Is this God's great joke? Does God give with one hand just to take away with the other?* Was this the end of that great pilgrimage of faith which started when Abraham responded to God's call in faith and left the security of Ur in Chaldea to set out for a promised land? And what about that promise God made to him and his wife, Sarah, that their descendants would be as plentiful as the stars in the heaven? A grim jest? The family line wiped out forever on that hill? Here is the first act in the drama, Abraham ascending heartbreak mountain.

The second part of the picture is in complete contrast. Now we can envisage the old man and the boy coming down the mountain. Old man? Why, he strides with the powerful, confident step of one years younger. There is a glint in his eyes. The boy skips by his side, delighting in his father's laughter and song. There on that hilltop a special bond was established between Abraham and God. Reverberating in his heart he can hear the word, which he knows came direct from heaven. "Do not lay your hand on the boy or do anything to him; for now I know that you fear God, since you have not withheld your son, your only son, from me" (Genesis 22:12). The words were like a song of redemption. More, they were a song of hope. God was revealed forever as the God of promise. The purposes at the heart of creation would be worked out through the kind of person represented by this towering figure in the story of faith. He held nothing back. He ascended the mountain chained to the past and its practices. He descends the mountain looking to the future with hope shining in his heart.

From that moment on, whenever God came to the early Hebrews, the announcement would be made: "I am the God of Abraham." God Almighty has not just a servant, not just a believer, not just a worshiper, but *a friend*. And here we trace the birth of a hope that this privileged relationship might become the destiny of all who were ready to hold nothing back in their worship and service.

W. E. Sangster tells (*The Pure in Heart,* Epworth Press, 1955; page 161) of an evangelistic mission that was held in York toward the end of the last century. One night, a number of people responded to the invitation, including an elderly man. The evangelist counseled each in turn, including this particular man, who meekly answered the questions put to him and then went his way. Later the evangelist learned that the elderly man was saintly David Hill, a most distinguished Methodist missionary in China who happened to be home on leave. (He would return shortly to the country he loved and die of typhus at Hankow.)

The preacher sought David Hill out and made a halting apology for having treated him as a beginner in the holy life. David Hill brushed his embarrassments aside. "I thought it would do me good to kneel among the penitents," he said. He had made it his practice never to hold anything back. He was a friend of God.

As we journey toward Christmastime and approach the Savior's cradle, the offering that God most desires is our heart's devotion. When we give that, holding nothing back, we join the select band of those who may be called "the friends of God."

6
The Touch of God

ased on Genesis 32:28

In our living room we have a corner cabinet with glass doors. It houses pieces of crystal given to us over the years. This modest collection includes things we treasure. In the center of the display there is something a visitor might consider out of place. It is a rather quaint, comic-looking china dog. I think it is supposed to be a poodle. It sits on its haunches with its front paws off the ground. Its cheeks are colored pale pink so that it appears to be blushing. It wears a funny-looking bonnet, which serves as a pin cushion. There is a slot on the bridge of its nose, which holds a small pair of scissors so that it appears to be wearing glasses. Its tail is a spring-loaded eighteen-inch tape measure.

Once when our house was broken into, the intruders took a number of objects they thought were worth something. They ignored the dog, which I can well understand. To them or anyone else, it has no value. To my wife and me, however, it is priceless. Whenever my medical career took us to another part of the country, we did not entrust that little dog to the tender care of the moving men. We did not mind their handling the rest of the glassware and china, but that strange creation was far too precious to be handled by any strangers. Instead it traveled with us, carefully protected from damage. Why does it merit such special protection? Any parent will understand the answer. When she was seven years of age, our daughter emptied her little piggy bank and, without any prompting from her parents, went to the local general store around the corner and bought it for our wedding anniversary. Something very ordinary was made extraordinary when touched by the grace and generosity of a little girl.

Some years ago, in the early hours of a January morning, I was called to the local hospital to baptize triplets who had been born prematurely. Their father, a distinguished scholarly man, aware that their hold on life was precarious, was most anxious that they should receive Christian baptism without delay. He stood beside his wife's wheelchair in the special care unit as I took some water and, reaching inside the incubators, made a cross on each of their tiny heads and said the words of the sacrament. What was so special about that water? To those of us there it had become more than water. The ordinary had become extraordinary because in faith we saw it touched by the grace and generosity of God and made a symbol and sign of Christian hope. Shortly afterward, as had been feared, the most frail one of those three tiny babies died. Once again I stood with the parents—this time in the hospital chapel—and reaffirmed that same hope in the glorious words, "We know that if our earthly house of this tabernacle were dissolved, we have a building of God, [a] house not made with hands, eternal in the heavens" (2 Corinthians 5:1 KJV).

The story of the faith is punctuated by ordinary individuals who became extraordinary because they were touched by God's grace and generosity and made symbols of hope.

When first introduced to us, some of them do not appear very promising, but as God begins the work of remolding, and as they respond to the divine touch, we see them becoming different people. Such a one was Jacob. As we see how he responded to God's touch, we can, perhaps, see also what God is doing to us as we make our Advent pilgrimage to Bethlehem. Jacob's story, like ours, may be regarded as a drama in three acts.

Act 1: God—A Stranger with Whom to Strike a Bargain

When we first meet him, Jacob is a shrewd, scheming individual motivated by self-interest. He does not hesitate to take advantage of his brother or deceive his aging father. Thus it is that early in his story Jacob has to flee from home, a fugitive escaping from the anger of his brother, Esau, whom Jacob has tricked out of his rightful inheritance.

One night, as Jacob travels to the safety of his grandfather's home, he rests at a place he later calls Bethel. There he has a strange dream in which he sees a ladder stretching from earth to heaven. A less spiritually sensitive person might have dismissed it as a figment of imagination, but Jacob believes that he has encountered God; and his first words the next morning impress us: "Surely the LORD is in this place—and I did not know it!... How awesome is this place! This is none other than the house of God, and this is the gate of heaven" (Genesis 28:16-17). But this good impression is soon shattered as the deceiver tries to strike a bargain with God. "If God will be with me... and will give me bread to eat and clothing to wear... *then* the LORD shall be my God" (Genesis 28:20, emphasis added). At this stage in his life, Jacob's allegiance and worship are conditional.

A. J. Cronin, in *The Keys of the Kingdom* (Victor Gollancz, 1942), describes how Francis Chisholm, a sincere, dedicated Catholic priest, was sent to China. On his arrival he found that the thriving mission he had been promised was nonexistent. Using his elementary medical knowledge, he opened a dispensary. This, at least, met with some response as people who were poor and sick came for help. One day Chisholm was dumbfounded when asked to go to see the six-year-old son of Mr. Chia, one of the wealthiest and most influential men of the region. He found the boy dying of septicemia from a grossly infected arm and hand. Risking the appalling consequences should he fail, Chisholm incised the infected limb and drained the life-threatening poison away. Almost immediately the boy started to mend. By his prompt action, Chisholm had saved the boy's life. Next day he returned to check on his patient's progress. As he was leaving, the priest was told that he did not need to come again. Firmly and politely he was dismissed from the case.

For days the priest struggled to quell his anger and indignation at such outrageous ingratitude. And then a week later, just as he was closing the dispensary, he was aware that Mr. Chia, the boy's father, was standing there. It was evidently a formal visit. Chia, dressed in his finest clothes, explained that he had not been able to come earlier because there was much to do. Now, at last, these other details had been dealt with and he had come. "Why?" asked Chisholm. "Naturally...to become a Christian" was the answer. Chia then went on to explain that although he did not believe, by becoming a Christian he would in some measure be repaying the debt he owed for his son's life. He was offering himself as his part of the bargain with Chisholm's God.

At that moment everything the priest longed for could have been his. Had Chia become a Christian, the rest of the town would have followed, and all Chisholm's problems would be over. There would be no shortage of financial support. Any opposition to the faith would be silenced by the rich man's servants. It was a prospect a lesser person would have eagerly seized. The priest, however, would have none of it. He rejected the offer; the God he served was not in the bargaining business. This was strange to Chia, who thought it natural to settle accounts and keep his end of a contract. He left the dispensary with his offer rejected but with a profound respect for this man of shining integrity, a respect that eventually led to a genuine conversion.

This is where Jacob is on his spiritual journey when he reaches Bethel. As we search our hearts on our seasonal journey to Bethlehem, we begin to realize that Jacob is not alone in trying to strike a bargain with God. Often our discipleship is conditional. Yes, we will go on believing, just as long as God keeps us and our loved ones in good health, guards our children from danger, enables our business to prosper, makes us popular with our friends, and provides us with the right partner. This Christmas season, God is prompting us to move on from this inadequate understanding to something more mature. We are urged to move on beyond Bethel.

Act 2: God—An Adversary with Whom It Is Necessary to Struggle

There is a Christian legend that in the town of Jericho, years after the death and resurrection of Jesus, the aged Zacchaeus used to slip out of his villa each morning and evening. According to the story he could be seen going to an outbuilding attached to the villa and emerging with a large earthenware jar. He would fill the jar with water from the well and then, with it on his shoulder, would make his way to the Jerusalem road. There he would lovingly pour the water around the roots of an old sycamore tree, and it was said that there was often the glimmer of tears on his cheeks. Once, when he was crouching beside the tree, someone who did not know his story saw the tears and asked him if he were feeling ill. The old man looked up at his questioner with a seraphic smile and replied, "I am quite well, thank you. But you see, it was here that I met Jesus."

Many people have special times and places where they

have been aware of the presence of God. For some it was quite unexpected; for others it came gradually in response to their search for a deeper dimension in their lives. Whether sudden or gradual, it was for them all a transforming encounter. After it happened, nothing could be the same again.

Jacob had such an experience. Years had passed since his treacherous deception of his brother. He had married and prospered. Now, returning to his home country with all his family, his flocks and herds, he heard the worrying news that Esau was coming to meet him with a large number of men. Jacob mistakenly feared that his brother still remembered how he had been deceived and was on his way to settle old scores.

That night, after his entire company had crossed a stream called Jabbok, Jacob had a strange experience that defied description and which has intrigued Bible students ever since. It seemed to him as though he was struggling with a man, but he then discovered that his adversary was in fact God. Although shrouded in mystery, it is clear that this was a transforming encounter. After it was over and his struggle with God the adversary was ended, Jacob was a different person. In awe he said, "I have seen God face to face, and yet my life is preserved" (Genesis 32:30).

A young man once came to Jesus. He had reached his Jabbok. "What must I do to inherit eternal life?" he asked. Jesus offered the way: "Sell what you own, and give the money to the poor...then come, follow me" (Mark 10:17-21). Here was a struggle in which Jesus was wrestling for this young man's soul and might have been seen as an adversary. In the end the will of the young man triumphed, but it was a hollow victory. He went away sorrowful and missed the greatest opportunity of his life.

There is a stage in our Advent journey when God appears as an adversary challenging all that is unworthy and base in our lives. If we can but see it, we have reached Jabbok. We struggle with our unseen adversary who challenges our self-ishness, greed, pride, love of power, and vanity. To surren-der and allow God to make us new by touching us with generosity and grace is to be prepared for an experience of the Christ Child. Without this, the celebration of the Savior's birth, instead of being a meaningful spiritual encounter, will be hollow, degenerating into yet another giddy whirl of spending and feasting. When God the adversary triumphs in this struggle for our souls, we become aware, with an over-whelming sense of wonder, that we are considered worth struggling for. Our journey through Advent to the cradle of the Christ Child prepares us for a transforming encounter when we kneel at the manger. Then with joy we will say what Zacchaeus said of the old tree: "It was here that I met Jesus."

Act 3: God—A Friend Who Journeys with Us

Ian Macpherson (*God's Middleman,* Epworth Press, 1965; page 74) relates how the poet Francis Thompson told of an Englishwoman whom a friend of his happened to meet in Paris. He was about to address her by name in company when the woman put up her hand restrainingly. "Hush!" she whispered. "Don't recognize me! I'm traveling in *embryo!*" Of course she had gotten the word wrong. She had intended to say "incognito." But without realizing it she was express-ing a profound truth. We are all traveling through life "in embryo." If we allow God to touch us with the grace and generosity displayed in the coming of the child of Bethlehem, we begin to develop into what the divine plan intended us to be.

For Jacob, the night has ended and his struggle with God is over. As dawn breaks there is still the stream to cross and the threat represented by Esau and his men to face. The future remains uncertain with all of its shadows and hurts. But there is now a tremendous difference. His spiritual embryo has undergone a momentous development. God has been experienced as a friend, and with that assurance Jacob travels with hope. This transforming encounter displays the wonder of faith, which looks beyond earth to heaven, beyond human weakness and despair to divine power and hope, beyond a cradle to a star. Jacob, the trickster who tried to bargain with God, has been touched by divine grace and generosity and is so changed that his old name *Jacob,* "the supplanter," is no longer appropriate. He is to be known as *Israel,* "the one who strives with God." The essential thing is not what Jacob *was* but what he *became* when touched by God; the ordinary made extraordinary.

The heart of the Christmas hope is that the God who transformed Jacob came in Jesus to transform the world, and one day that transformation will be complete.

At the church a friend of mine was serving in the north of England, the choir always performed Handel's *Messiah* during Advent. In his final year there, the musical director told him that the soprano soloist he had engaged was blind. My friend's immediate thoughts were of the practical details that would need attention. He arranged for someone to help her up the steps to the platform since she would be in unfamiliar surroundings. The tenor soloist who would be sitting next to her was asked to make sure that she knew where to stand when she sang. The chair selected for her had arms so that she could feel for them as she sat down. Everything had been meticulously planned. My friend said that his mind was not on the performance but on the possibility of some small problem arising.

Then, on the night of the performance, during its progress, he found himself suddenly lifted to the heavens. It happened at the point where the soprano and the contralto soloists have to rise together. The choir had just proclaimed in music the glorious fulfillment of prophecy that a child had been born who would be called the prince of peace. The blind soprano then sang in ringing tones, "Rejoice, rejoice greatly O daughter of Zion." As though to expound this message, the contralto gently sang, "Then shall the eyes of the blind be opened and the tongue of the dumb sing.... He shall feed his flock like a shepherd," to which the blind soprano responded, "Come unto him all ye that labor and he will give you rest."

Here was the testimony of one who had a right to speak. Because of her blindness, she might have been denied a thousand things others take for granted, but she could rejoice greatly. One day the eyes of the blind *would* be opened. One day the tongue of the mute *would* sing. One day the God who changed a man such as Jacob *would* complete the work and change the world. This is the hope of this glorious season. But God begins by touching and changing us.

7

David's Line

ased on Ruth 4:15

As Christmas draws near, hearts and minds turn to remember with gladness the Savior's first coming in Bethlehem long ago. Christians rejoice because of the Advent hope that one day there will be a glorious Messianic return in majesty and power.

For many, however, as Christmas draws near, the rejoicing is swamped by a rising tide of panic. How can everything possibly be done in time for the festival? The tree isn't up yet. There are still so many presents to buy. The cards have not been written. There are rehearsals at the church for the Nativity pageant. The scattered members of the family will be returning in just over a week, and we are nowhere near ready. The days are passing far too quickly. If only time would slow down!

How different when we were children. Then, December seemed to last forever. "How many days to Christmas?" I asked several times each day. Patiently my mother would take me to the calendar hanging on the wall and show me how each day was crossed off at its close. "When we come to 24, you will know it is Christmas Eve and time to hang up your stocking," she would say.

To ease our ache of waiting for Christmas, during the evenings of Advent my mother would gather us around her knee by the fire and tell stories. Our favorites were her memories of Christmas spent with her grandparents when she was young. Her eyes sparkled as she recalled how her grandparents, though poor in material things, were wonderfully rich toward God. Little did she realize that in describing to my sensitive mind my two devout forebears she was painting word pictures that would adorn the gallery of my memory all my life. Each year at this time I walk through that gallery, and as I think of my great-grandparents, I am reminded of my rich heritage of faith.

I wonder if that happened to young David? He was the boy destined to become Israel's greatest king. His reign would be recalled by later ages as being a foretaste of the great Messianic age. When Zechariah, the father of John the Baptist, was expressing his thanksgiving to God he said, "Blessed be the Lord God of Israel, / for he has looked favorably on his people and redeemed them. / He has raised up a mighty savior for us / *in the house of his servant David*" (Luke 1:68-69, emphasis added). God's great deliverer was promised to be "of David's line," and the name of this outstanding king is featured in many of our Advent hymns. What pictures did David's father, Jesse, hang in the gallery of the child's sensitive mind? I feel sure that in the light of the flickering fire Jesse would have recalled David's great-grandmother, a remarkable woman who across the ages has been honored as one of the great figures in the story of faith. Few of us have not been moved by the lovely story of Ruth, who came from the land of Moab.

As Christians, we rejoice in the knowledge that in the little town of Bethlehem, God was about to fulfill the promise of bringing us a deliverer from evil. As we have been reminded already, however, this promise did not begin in Roman-occupied Judea when Herod was king. We have seen how, long before the star guided wise men to the cradle, God was carefully laying the foundation of hope in the tents of Abraham and Jacob. In those same fields around Bethlehem where one day shepherds would hear the angelic announcement of the Savior's birth, young David played, and Ruth, his great-grandmother, followed the reapers, gleaning grain.

It is fitting that on our journey to the cradle of the one who was to be born of David's line, the spotlight should shine for a brief time upon Ruth, this remarkable woman who came from a foreign land. Advent—the season of prayer and preparation before Christmas—is the time when we anticipate the fulfillment of all the prophetic promises and the final victory of suffering love. Living each day as though it could be the day when Christ will come and bring in that Messianic age is what makes Advent people. If we would join their number, then Ruth can be our guide.

Advent People Can Be Identified by the Quality of Their Living

Ruth reminds us that to be an "Advent person" involves much more than merely *saying* the right things. Actions speak louder than words. Expensive gifts at Christmas cannot make up for the pain caused to others by being harsh, unkind, and thoughtless. If we are to live in the spirit of Advent, then, not for a brief season only but throughout the year, our lives must have about them a quality that indicates that we are ready for the coming of Christ.

Once when he was preaching in the Cambridge University church, Billy Graham began by recalling a newspaper reporter's question. He had been asked whether or not he thought his sermons had accomplished anything. He disarmed his questioner by humorously relating an incident that had happened to him while on a flight to North Carolina (*Sermons from Great St. Mary's,* ed. High Montefiore, Collins, Fontana Books, 1968). On the plane was a man who was intoxicated. The man's language and conduct were very undesirable. Eventually it was necessary for the flight attendant to call for the assistance of the copilot in order to persuade him to resume his seat. The Reverend Graham said, "Someone whispered to the drunken man that I was sitting behind him. He got himself up again, turned around, and said to me, 'Are you Billy Graham?' I said 'Yes.' Then he said, 'I want to shake hands with you because your sermons have sure helped me.'"

The great evangelist then went on to describe, in contrast, how the church was built not upon empty professions such as that of the man on the plane but upon lives that had been transformed by the impact of the spirit of God. Not just words, but deeds mark men and women as Advent people.

Few passages in all literature can match the words Ruth addressed to her mother-in-law, Naomi, when Naomi decided to return to her home in Judea. Years before, during a time of famine, Naomi with her husband and two sons had left their home and had sought refuge in the foreign land of Moab. After the death of Naomi's husband, her sons fell in love and married local women. A bond of deep affection was forged between the widowed mother and her two daughters-in-law. Then, after the loss of her husband, calamity struck Naomi again. One after the other, her two sons died. Overwhelmed by grief she decided to return to her old home in Bethlehem. When she announced this intention, her two daughters-in-law insisted on going with her. Naomi felt sure that they would have a better chance to rebuild their lives in their own country of Moab and begged them to return to the homes of their parents. One reluctantly followed her advice. Ruth, however, was immovable and in immortal words, exquisitely expressed by the old King James Version, said:

Entreat me not to leave thee, or to return from following after thee: for whither thou goest, I will go; and where thou lodgest, I will lodge: thy people shall be my people, and thy God my God: Where thou diest, will I die, and there will I be buried: the LORD do so to me, and more also, if aught but death part thee and me. (Ruth 1:16-17 KJV)

These were noble sentiments. For Ruth, however, they were more than just talk. She robed her words with deeds. Despite the natural reluctance of the people of Bethlehem to accept a foreigner, she stayed by Naomi's side. She did not shrink from lowly work such as gleaning in the fields for grain so that she and her mother-in-law might eat. The story had a happy ending as Ruth married Boaz, a local landowner and kinsman, and, in due time, gave birth to a son. The compliments the local women paid Naomi on having a grandson were all the more powerful because of their earlier suspicions of the stranger from another country. "Your daughter-in-law who loves you, *who is more to you than seven sons,* has borne him" (Ruth 4:15, emphasis added).

David had a worthy great-grandmother. And when Jesus is hailed in our singing as "Great David's greater Son," we call to mind that his descent can be traced back to one who by the quality of her life expressed the meaning of Advent living.

Advent People Can Be Identified by the Quality of Their Loving

When Ruth accompanied her mother-in-law on that sad journey back to Bethlehem she had no thought for herself. The future was a closed book. In her devotion to Naomi she was not following some hidden agenda of self-interest. Out of love she wanted only to give. There is no mention in her story of any sense of personal loss, still less self-pity or bitterness, even though her husband had been snatched from her when they were both still young. Her own hurts had been swallowed up in self-giving.

Advent is the season when we recall the self-giving of God. Paul quotes an early Christian hymn about Jesus, which says "though he was in the form of God, / [he] did not regard equality with God / as something to be exploited, / but emptied himself, / taking the form of a slave, / being born in human likeness" (Philippians 2:6-7). Jesus taught that they who are prepared to lose their lives in loving service truly find the meaning of life. At Advent and Christmas, we remember with gratitude how the promised One "of David's line" fulfilled the hope that a reign of love would be established, putting an end to the night of hatred and enmity. Centuries earlier, David's great-grandmother Ruth, by her self-giving love, kept this hope alive during a dark period in the nation's life. In losing herself in service, she found herself. And this is the secret of Advent loving.

A formative influence on my life was a Bible class for boys, which I attended each Sunday afternoon. We were a rowdy bunch, and our teacher was a gracious, refined lady whom we knew as Miss Johnson. We thought of her as middle-aged. Looking back, I realize that she was probably in her early twenties! In our boisterous and thoughtless behavior, I fear that we must have taken unfair advantage of her quiet patience.

One Sunday in June 1944 we were particularly noisy. Exciting things were happening. During the preceding week all the trucks and tanks and the tens of thousands of American soldiers, who had been crowded into our town and the surrounding countryside of that part of England, had disappeared as if by magic. Then we heard the news. On June 6, the Allies had launched the massive invasion of Normandy. We were all talking about this at the tops of our voices on that second Sunday afternoon in June when Miss Johnson arrived. She took her seat behind the table, and after an opening prayer she opened her Bible. Her voice was particularly soft, and she spoke unusually slowly. We were seated around the table in a semicircle. One of our number had brought a bag of marbles. Miss Johnson had scarcely begun the lesson when he rolled one of them across the floor to the person on the other side of the semicircle, and that person rolled it back. We all thought this was hilarious. Soon, marbles were rolling in all directions. Miss Johnson then did something she had never done before. She closed her Bible and rose to her feet. In a trembling voice she said, "Boys, you are in no mood for Bible study this afternoon. I am going to say a prayer and then go home." We were instantly subdued. We knew we had gone too far. As she made her way to the door, we could see that Miss Johnson's cheeks were wet with tears.

Next Sunday we gathered at the usual time for the Bible class, feeling quite sure that Miss Johnson would not turn up after our misconduct the week before. We were wrong. She came, on time as usual. The week after that, she came. Similarly, the week after that. Regularly, without a break, she continued to lead that class. Miss Johnson never married. Several years later I discovered by chance that her fiancé had been killed on the Normandy beaches during that fateful invasion for the liberation of Europe. She had come to the class on that particular Sunday having just received the news. Her heart was breaking. But instead of allowing self-pity or bitterness to overwhelm her, she lost herself in loving service for the sake of some silly, ill-behaved boys who thought it was clever to roll marbles when she was trying to teach. It is because of such as her that I came to faith. She showed me what Advent loving was all about.

This is a lesson we can all learn from Ruth, the great-grandmother of David. During a dark period in her life, self-giving love shone through the gloom and filled that home in Bethlehem with a radiant light. And, in the fullness of time, the prophetic promises have been fulfilled in one who was born "of David's line." Through Jesus a new race of people has come into being. They live as though each day is the day when the Messianic age will begin. They can be distinguished because of the quality of their loving.

Ian Macpherson tells (*News of the World to Come*, Prophetic Witness Publishing House, 1975; page 296) of a visitor touring Switzerland who saw on the shore of a beautiful lake a delightful mansion. He was deeply impressed by the large and perfectly kept garden in which it was set. The close-cropped lawns, trim and tidy paths and terraces, and gorgeous flower beds were testimony to loving and unremitting toil on the part of the gardening staff. Not a weed was to be seen anywhere. The tourist paused to admire the scene and, seeing one of the staff, the curator, there in the garden, he praised its order and beauty to him. "How long have you worked here?" he asked. "Twenty years," was the reply. In the conversation that followed, it was disclosed that the owner of the mansion was absent most of the time. "How often has the owner been in residence during your twenty years of service?" the tourist asked. "Four times," replied the curator. The visitor expressed his surprise. "And to think," he exclaimed, "that for all these years you have kept this house and garden in such superb condition! Why, you look after them just as if you expected your master to come tomorrow!" "No," corrected the curator, "I look after things as if I expected my master to come today!"

This is a picture of Advent people. You can tell who they are. They live and love each day as if it were the day of their Savior's coming.

8

Mary's Boy Child

ased on Luke 2:7

In my youth I heard a preacher tell of an old Englishman
who fell on hard times and was compelled to sell his small
collection of coins. He asked a dealer to visit his house and
give an appraisal. The dealer came and sniffed around the
old man's treasures. Then, in a condescending manner, he
said, "I'll give you five pounds (eight dollars) for the lot."
The face of the old man fell. He had not expected much, but
he had thought his collection was more valuable than that.
Then the dealer turned and pointed to something hanging
on a nail in the wall. It was just a piece of bronze attached
to a colored ribbon. "But I'll give you a hundred pounds for
that," he said. The old man's demeanor changed. He stood
erect and went over to the piece of bronze, which was fash-
ioned in the shape of a cross. He fondled it proudly. Things
might be tough but they were not as bad as that. What he
held in his hands was the Victoria Cross, the highest honor
for gallantry that his grateful country could bestow. "I'll not

part with that," he said. "My king pinned that medal on my chest." Only a piece of bronze! But it was a precious symbol more important to that man than food or drink.

Symbols help us to express the inexpressible. This is why the Christian faith—and especially the Christmas story—is so rich in them. The stable, the manger, the innocent young mother, the helpless infant Jesus—all send out powerful visual messages that help us grasp a little of the meaning of two of the most colossal words that, as we have already seen, lie at the heart of our faith.

The first of these words is *immanence*—the conviction that God is not "out there" but here, among us, down where we live. At heart we are all like the child who asked his parents where God was. When his father replied, "God is everywhere," the child said, "But I want God to be *somewhere*." In response to this longing to see God, Christmas calls out, "Hurry to Bethlehem! When you look at the baby in the manger, you are looking at God." The cradle is the symbol of God's immanence. *Emmanuel* means "God with us."

The second of these two words is *transcendence*. God is hid in light and is beyond the grasp of human reason. We cannot fathom the mystery of the Holy One, the Creator. The star that is far beyond us is a symbol of this "otherness" of God.

As we travel now to Bethlehem, we find these two tremendous concepts, symbolized by the cradle and the star, brought together as a baby rests in the arms of young, humble, obedient Mary. Here the symbols help us to understand the thrilling eternal truths that are bound up in these two great words of faith.

The Call of Bethlehem—to Wonder at God's Love Expressed in Human Form

When I was about twelve years old, I was taken to my first philharmonic concert. It was produced specially for school-children. "You are in for a treat," our music teacher said enthusiastically. "You will hear a great orchestra and one of the finest choirs in the country." The bus taking us to the city where the concert was to be held was delayed. We arrived at the last minute, and, breathless with anticipation, I took my seat in the balcony. I absorbed the scene in wonder. The vast choir was already in place. On the platform were men and women playing instruments the like of which I had never seen before, but this was not my idea of music, and soon my glee had changed to terrible disappointment. What a let-down! At that moment I did not realize that what I thought was the first number was in fact merely the orchestra tuning up!

And then an expectant hush descended upon the packed hall. The choir rose, and this was the signal for the audience to erupt into applause as the distinguished conductor, immaculate in his formal suit, a white carnation in his button-hole, made his entrance. He took his place on the rostrum, tapped with his baton, and pointed to the timpani. They rolled, and suddenly orchestra and choir filled the air with the majestic music of the national anthem. It was spine-tinglingly thrilling! I had never heard anything like it before, and for the rest of the program I was spellbound. From that moment on, music became a vital part of my life.

In the fields outside Bethlehem an angel delivered the announcement of the Savior's birth. The concluding words of the message were like a baton brought down to signal all the host of heaven to burst into song. And what were these words? *"This shall be a sign unto you; ye shall find the babe wrapped in swaddling clothes, lying in a manger."* That was it! Luke then goes on to say, *"And suddenly there was with the angel a multitude of the heavenly host praising God"* (Luke 2:12-13 KJV).

It would have been a momentous thing had God come to rule robed in glory and majesty. But heaven bursts into rapture because God did something even more wonderful. The Holy One came as a baby, slept in a manger, and lay in the warmest of cradles, the arms of a loving mother. God Almighty reached out tiny fingers to touch, whimpered when hungry, and became utterly dependent upon a young woman's care. Here we have displayed the immanence of God, who became vulnerable and one of us. Some years later, in one of the greatest Christian works ever penned, John the apostle would describe this event in imperishable words: "And the Word became flesh and lived among us, and we have seen his glory, the glory as of a father's only son, full of grace and truth" (John 1:14).

Our joy in the Savior's birth is tempered, however, by a sense of awe and even of sorrow. Another symbol rises in our minds alongside those of cradle and star. It is the symbol of a cross upon a hill. The sublime event of this baby's birth is part of God's great redemptive plan, which is destined to include pain and desolation. Before God's purpose is accomplished, Mary will have earned the name later ages would give her, "Mother of Sorrows." Christian art offers us two pictures of her holding her son. In the first she is cradling Jesus as a baby, and we can almost hear her singing a lullaby. In the second, the *Pietà*, she has across her lap his lifeless form after the Crucifixion. The road from Bethlehem will lead to Calvary, where, as Paul expresses it, "in Christ God was reconciling the world to himself."

In one of the Sunday school rooms of the church in which I was brought up, there was a print of one of Holman Hunt's most famous paintings, *The Shadow of Death*. It depicts Jesus as a young man who has completed his work at the carpenter's bench for the day. He is standing, stretching his limbs for relief after being cramped up. His arms are outstretched, and the sun throws the shadow of his form on the wall behind him, and it looks like a cross. The artist is saying through his picture that the cross was there before Jesus began to preach in Galilee. Of course Holman Hunt was right, but the truth is that the cross was there much earlier. In an eighteenth-century Christmas hymn, one stanza says:

Like Mary, let us ponder in our mind
God's wondrous love in saving lost mankind;
Trace we the Babe, who has retrieved our loss,
From the poor manger to the bitter cross.
              (*John Byrom, 1692–1763*)

Bethlehem calls us to wonder. Here is set before our eyes the amazing love of God's redemptive plan. Only by taking human form could God redeem a lost humanity. The cradle points to a divine love willing to take this incomprehensible step, lay aside all the glory of divinity, and become a baby. The transcendent God becoming wondrously immanent. God with us. No wonder the hosts of heaven sang!

The Comfort of Bethlehem—to Rejoice in Everlasting Hope

Christmas is about two decrees and two books.

The first decree was issued from the court of Augustus, Emperor of Rome, the most powerful man alive. He decreed that the world should be enrolled for tax purposes, and his legions saw to it that his word was obeyed. The names of all Roman subjects were thus duly entered in Caesar's book.

The second decree was issued not from a human court but from the court of heaven. It declared that God planned for all people to be enrolled in another book—the Book of Life. Unlike Caesar's book, this would not be transient but eternal. On that first Christmas night, to those living at that time, it must have seemed that all might and power belonged to Augustus. History, however, has handed down a different verdict. It is ironic that the great Caesar Augustus is now remembered by most people only because of the part he played in the story of that baby nursed by a peasant girl in a stable. Caesar in Rome represents *the transient;* the baby resting in his mother's arms represents *the eternal.*

I love Christmas! With festive decorations throughout the

house, I find it a joyful time. We are not embarrassed at our childlike delight in receiving seasonal greetings from friends far and near. Each one is cherished. We eagerly read the glad news these messages bring: a new baby, a wedding in the family, or, perhaps, new grandchildren. Our Christmas joy is enhanced by sharing the gladness of our friends.

But other messages also arrive in the mail during this season. We open a Christmas envelope and find, with the card, a note that tells a different story. It happens every year. Indeed, two such messages came this very morning. The first read: "You will be sorry to hear that two months ago Arthur died." The second in the same mail carried the words, "We have been stunned by the loss of our darling daughter just six weeks ago." Suddenly we find ourselves on a roller coaster of emotion. From laughter we are plunged into tears. The song of the angels is hushed and the lights of Christmas are dimmed as we glimpse into the dark abyss of death. Our frail hearts whisper, "Is this the end?"

My mother-in-law died suddenly one Christmas. She was relatively young, and naturally we were overwhelmed with sorrow. Loving friends expressed concern that so dark a shadow had been cast upon such a happy season. We were greatly helped by what someone wrote who looked at this sad event from a different perspective. "Do not think of the shadow which this sorrow has cast over your Christmas," he said. "Think rather of the light which Christmas sheds upon this sorrow." Advent hope! God's eternal promise which first brought that hope to birth long ago, as we have seen in the tents of Abraham and Isaac and in the gleaning fields with Ruth, has reached its glorious fulfillment in the coming of Jesus.

The cradle and the star, symbols of God's immanence and transcendence, stand before us in our sorrow, our fear, and our pain. They beckon us to look to God, to discover in the transient events of Bethlehem an everlasting significance. Here, God has stepped decisively into human affairs and, in doing so, has defeated death and all other terrors. We can, therefore, bring our tired and frightened spirits to the crib of the Christ Child and there find comfort. Then we discover not only Advent *hope* but also Advent *joy*.

The Challenge of Bethlehem—to Become Part of God's Grand Design

Huckleberry Finn tells us that when the Widow Douglas told him about Moses and the bulrushes he was in quite a sweat to find out all about him. But author Mark Twain goes on to relate that when Huckleberry Finn discovered that Moses had been dead for a long time, he was able to dismiss the story from his mind. "I don't take no stock in dead people," Huckleberry said. Since it was just history, he did not need to concern himself about it.

The delightful nativity pageants, in which characters appear in the costume of biblical times, give us a comforting sense of distance. We find it so easy to be like Huckleberry Finn and think of the story of the birth of Jesus as just history. Then there is no need for us to get into a sweat about it. But to find such complacent peace of mind, we must avoid thinking about Mary. She is disturbing, even frightening, and she stabs our spirits broad awake. Her willingness, in all her youthful innocence, to become part of God's grand design for the salvation of the world, even though it would involve shame, humiliation, and the unkind gossiping tongues of Nazareth, shatters our easygoing complacency. Mary becomes more than history. She becomes a symbol of the life of faith which, if it is to be real, must be embodied in commitment and obedience.

A preacher friend of mine used to tell of a man who, on his way to his office, passed a building site where the new headquarters of a large bank was being erected. As a hobby this man worked in stone, and therefore, he was particularly interested in a stonemason who was chiseling at a piece of marble. He paused to watch, but the craftsman was too engrossed in his work to notice him. Each day as he passed, he would pause to see how the work progressed, and to admire the work of the stonemason. One morning, as he watched, the stonemason happened to look up, and their eyes met. The onlooker smiled and complimented the craftsman on his work. The other nodded his thanks. "Where will this piece of marble fit when you have finished your work?" the onlooker asked. "I don't know," the mason replied. "I haven't seen the plans. I just trust the architect and do my part as best I can."

Mary did not know the whole of God's wondrous redemptive plan. What she did know was that there was a part in it for her, and in faithful obedience she was ready to play that part to the full. She demonstrated her faith not through fine-sounding words but in placing her whole self at the disposal of God. She shines out in a world of compromise as a symbol of complete commitment to the divine will.

No passage of scripture is more powerful than Mary's song (Luke 1:46-55). She reaches back into the history of her people and links the promises given to past ages with what was about to happen in her life. "[God] has helped his servant Israel [Jacob], / in remembrance of his mercy, / according to the promise he made to our ancestors, / to Abraham and to his descendants forever" (Luke 1:54-55). But she does more than just look back across the centuries. With the eye of faith she looks into the future, beyond the birth of the Savior to the end of history when God will end the injustices of the ages and establish a rule of righteousness.

Mary accepted the challenge to become part of God's grand design and allow her life to be used. She challenges us as we journey toward Bethlehem to follow her example and allow God to use us to bring nearer the fulfillment of the divine will. The test of our commitment to God's plan is to be seen not in our words but in our deeds. It is what we *are*, not merely what we *say*, which is the real test.

In his book *What Is a Christian* (Abingdon Press, 1962; page 21), Leonard Griffith tells how one day the philosopher Josiah Royce was sitting in his study at Harvard University talking with a young student. In the course of the conversation the student asked the professor, "What is your definition of a Christian?" The great philosopher replied, "I do not know how to define a Christian.... But wait," he added, looking out the window, "there goes Phillips Brooks." What he was saying was that you cannot define Christianity in words; it must be embodied in a life, and this man so lived the life of faith that he had become part of God's plan to establish the reign of love and righteousness. He was an Advent person.

Early in his ministry, Phillips Brooks visited the Holy Land and chanced to be in Bethlehem on Christmas Day. As a result, in this season, Christians all over the world who know nothing of his historic ministry in Boston are blessed through the words he was moved to write while there:

O little town of Bethlehem, how still we see thee lie;
Above thy deep and dreamless sleep the silent stars go by.
Yet in thy dark streets shineth the everlasting light;
The hopes and fears of all the years are met in thee tonight.

Above all our hopes and fears we placed the cradle and the star to remind us of God's immanence and transcendence. These two symbols come together at Bethlehem to call us to wonder, to comfort us with a glimpse of the eternal, and to challenge us to take part in carrying out God's design. Let our response to this wondrous event be to offer our lives in homage at the manger, and Christ will be reborn in us. If this happens, our celebration will become a time of spiritual renewal and our Advent journey will end with a Christmas experience that is gloriously different!

REFLECTION
Nell W. Mohney

od so loved the world, that he gave his only begotten son that whosoever believeth in him should not perish, but have everlasting life.
—John 3:16 KJV

At Christmastime each year something magical seems to happen. It's evidenced in the livelier way we walk, in our smiles and our generosity. It is enhanced by the sound of Christmas carols, the dancing eyes of little children, candlelit homes and church services, the smell of fruitcake baking, and snow flurries.

This season is the time for giving because of God's great gift in Jesus Christ. Let us ask ourselves two questions: Have we received God's gift personally? What are we giving others in gratitude for God's gift?

In addition to our beautifully wrapped and ribbon-tied packages, what are the intangible gifts that will make a significant difference in the lives of others?

PART THREE

The Christmas People

J. Ellsworth Kalas

INTRODUCTION

A t this time of the year, we are asked to prepare our hearts for the Christmas celebration by realizing what the world would be like if Christ had not come. In a sense, this is an artificial exercise, because we know that Jesus *has* come. Indeed, considering the piped-in music in every shopping mall, it would be impossible to think otherwise. For although it seems to grow more secular every year, this mall music still includes enough traditional Christmas songs (and enough substantial Christian theology) to unnerve any secular shopper who really hears.

But truly preparing for the celebration of the birth of Christ is a good exercise, nevertheless; and a very important one, in fact, because it reminds us that a great number of people—perhaps even a majority—don't really know that Christ has come. For them, the angels may be singing just outside, and the wise men may be walking their street, but they live in a world that the prophet Isaiah described as one where "the people . . . walked in darkness" (Isaiah 9:2). We ought to ponder this and be moved to share the good news that we have experienced.

And in truth, even those of us who call ourselves believers have times when we live, work, and think as if Jesus had not come. At such times, we need to remind ourselves of the difference our Lord's coming has made in our lives.

This season of the year is meant to bring new depth of meaning to our own sense of Christmas-realized.

In the pages that follow, we will journey into the familiar world of Christmas as we know it—the world of lonely people, of harried workers, of spendthrift shoppers, and of the sometimes unnoticed saints—in order to remind us that it is for such a world as this that our Lord was born.

With that new realization, I pray that we will experience the meaning of Christmas with a new measure of love and joy; and that having received such a blessing, we will share this love and joy extravagantly with a generation that needs it so profoundly.

9

Christmas Is for Lonely People

based on Isaiah 9:1-7

The Christmas season is the happiest time of the year. We say it and sing it, so it must be so. But unfortunately, many people will say—if they get a chance—that Christmas is the *loneliest* time of the year. Some data seem to support this view. There are a disturbing number of suicides during the Christmas holiday season; and as the year draws to a close, psychiatrists often experience an increase in the number of cases of persons with severe depression. Christmas may be the loveliest time of the year—and potentially the happiest—but for some, it is also the loneliest.

It's easy to see why this is true. On a very practical level, Christmas is the season of memories. It's a time when the computer of our souls plays back an endless series of episodes from other days. Often these are beautiful memories, but there's something peculiar in our human psyche that tells us that the present is not as wonderful as those good old days, and that the future will never quite be able to duplicate such wonder.

Christmas memories also include times of special pain, and this pain usually returns with exquisite strength during this season. Those who are bereaved recall the Christmases when the circle of love was complete. The pain of having lost a loved one subsides at some points during the year, but it returns in full power during the holiday season. So, too, with persons who have gone through a divorce: At other times of the year, they may reason that they're better off as they are; but at Christmas, a certain mellowness often sets in, the feeling that "it really wasn't so bad then. We had lots of good times. I miss the way things used to be." This is the nature of the special pain that Christmas can bring.

Sometimes, ironically, the lonely feeling comes during this season simply because it seems that everyone else is so *happy*. Self-pity whispers, "You're the only unhappy person in the whole world." At such a moment, if you can only find someone else who is unhappy, you immediately feel better! And, probably, some of the loneliness comes simply from trying too hard. We go to so many events, work so hard to prepare, want so much to please others and ourselves that we are overcome by sheer exhaustion. Ennui—the tendency to be dissatisfied and bored—says, "What's the purpose of it all, and is it worth it?"

These feelings are very real and very valid. But the phenomenon of Christmas loneliness goes much deeper. Indeed, it is so much at the heart of our human condition that I am bold to say that Christmas came to deal with the very fact of human loneliness. That is, Christmas is *especially* for lonely people.

Christmas is often touched by a certain feeling of homesickness. This isn't surprising when you consider that so many of our Christmas delights are related to home. An old friend of mine, George F. Strickling, sat in the St. Paul, Minnesota, railroad station at Christmas vacation time in 1925 and wrote a poem he called "Waiting Room Blues." It spoke of those "dear loved ones" who were "left so far behind."

In his book *An Old-Fashioned Christmas* (Dial Press, 1964), Paul Engle tells of his experience one December twenty-third when he was at Kennedy International Airport in New York City during a snowstorm. He says that as he walked past small groups of anxious, waiting people, he repeatedly overheard the same phrase: "home with the family by Christmas." Engle goes on to say that this is true only of Christmas: We don't desperately try to rush home for the Fourth of July; only Christmas holds such a family attraction. Then he grows philosophical and says, "This is as it should be, for the original event on a cold desert night of conspicuous stars was a family affair."

Professor Engle is on the right track, though I want to take the matter further than he may have had in mind. The homesickness of the Christmas season is more than just a human story. It is more than the memories of childhood, more than the poignant recalling of happy days long past. It is the homesickness of the human soul, and it reaches all the way back to the Garden of Eden. There is an eternal thing in us, as old as the human race itself, that knows we have wandered from home. Some people try to persuade us otherwise, telling us that we are only time-bound creatures conceived in a womb and doomed to end in a tomb; but all of us instinctively know better. Sometimes we may wish that we were not eternal, that we could erase this longing for Eden, but it is impossible to change what we so profoundly are. Every time we have some rush of homesickness—for old friends, for family, for grade school or college, for the old neighborhood—it is a homesickness informed by our longing for Eden. G. K. Chesterton, the British novelist, essayist, and critic, put it perfectly:

> For men are homesick in their homes,
>   And strangers under the sun,
> And they lay their heads in a foreign land
>   Whenever the day is done.
> ("The House of Christmas")

Another eternal quality of loneliness in Christmas—also related to the matter of homesickness—has peculiar factors of its own. I'm referring to the matter of our unfulfilled dreams. I speak not simply of the dream to be president or an All-American athlete or a millionaire, or to find a frog and discover he or she is a prince or princess. I speak of the dreamer within each of us that is responsible for all of these coherent (even if sometimes absurd) dreams. We are dreamers by definition. The anthropologist says that we humans are creatures with opposable thumbs; I want to add that we are creatures who dream. Students of sleep say that most of us dream intermittently throughout much of the night. I am more impressed by the dreams that fill our waking hours, the sometimes lovely, sometimes aching hopes, fantasies, and expectations that pursue us.

Where do these dreams come from? What makes us reach for that which is out of reach? Why does the young girl in the heartland think that she could be the next teen singing sensation? Why does the little boy on the school playground think he will someday be the National Basketball Association's most valuable player? Where do we get our dreams?

But more significant, what is the nature and quality of those dreams that we cannot even put into words? We human beings have longings that defy verbalization. Once in a while, a poet or a novelist is able to write down words that catch something of the feeling, or a composer transcribes some haunting refrain—perhaps a lost chord—that evokes the feeling. But most of the time, we can find no way to express what we so deeply, ineffaceably feel, a dream of beauty and wholeness that is indescribable and that begins to lose its reality as soon as we try to wrap it in words. Where did we get such dreams? How can we long so much for something we've never seen or experienced?

Again, this kind of longing is as old as the human race. It is part of our hunger for the divine image we have lost. It reaches back to ancient Eden. And it makes us lonely twice over: first, because in such moments we feel alone within the human race. It's hard to believe that anyone else could have such a deep desire as this. And second, because it makes us feel isolated even from our own psyche. We are possessed by a dream that we ourselves don't understand, so that we feel almost as if another person were also inhabiting our skin, a person we don't really know, even though he or she bears the same name. This makes for a kind of ultimate loneliness.

And Christmas, by its very nature, awakens and makes more painfully sensitive this whole unfulfilled dream. Imagine this: You are walking to the center of a shopping mall as evening begins to fall. Some workers and shoppers are hurrying to buses and parking lots. Christmas decorations shine merrily, and Christmas music fills the air. But then suddenly, in the midst of all this busy, pleasant activity, you are overcome by a sense of the Christmas loneliness of the human race. Even those who scorn Christmas can't fully escape it; even Scrooge is troubled by it. We want to believe that next year will be better, that our best human dreams, both personal and general, will be fulfilled. And in that moment of longing, we are made lonely.

And here's why: because *Christmas is the answer to our eternal homesickness, and it is the beginning of the fulfillment of our longings and our impossible dreams.* The prophet Isaiah put this idea into words more than twenty-five hundred years ago. In a time very different from ours—yet, in its human qualities, so much the same—Isaiah said:

> The people who walked in darkness
>   have seen a great light;
> those who lived in a land of deep darkness—
>   on them light has shined.   (Isaiah 9:2)

Isaiah recognized the darkness of our human condition, and he envisioned the breaking forth of redeeming light. Here is how he saw that light coming:

> For a child has been born for us,
>   a son given to us;
> authority rests upon his shoulders;
>   and he is named
> Wonderful Counselor, Mighty God,
>   Everlasting Father, Prince of Peace. (Isaiah 9:6)

The basic loneliness of the human heart is the loneliness of displaced persons—of persons, that is, who were meant to live in Eden but who instead find themselves at a distance from God. And it is the loneliness of unfulfilled dreams, the dreams of persons who were meant to live in the image of God but who instead struggle with failure and frailty. We are a people who were meant to hear the music of heaven but who are forced most of the time to cope with the dissonance of earth.

Christmas comes to heal that basic human loneliness. Jesus Christ visited our world to bring us back to God; to bring us Home. G. K. Chesterton expresses this beautifully:

> A Child in a foul stable,
>   Where the beasts feed and foam;
> Only where He was homeless
>   Are you and I at home.
>   ("The House of Christmas")

There was, you see, a world of lonely people who had wandered from home. But these people could never forget the dream and could never lose their taste for home. So Jesus came to this world to say to all the lonely ones, "You can come Home. The heavenly Father wants you, and I will show you the way."

So Christmas comes, especially and profoundly, for lonely people. It invades our loneliness with love and light. This is why there was a star, and the angel song, and a birth in Bethlehem: because God cared about the lonely, and he sent his Son to find them and to save them.

10
Christmas Is
for Workers

ased on Luke 2:8-20

The Christmas season means laughter and festivities; it means social events and celebrations, and pausing before too many tables of cookies and candy and punch. It's such a relaxing, sociable time that we're likely to think Christmas is for those who *play*. And in some ways, of course, it *is*. But from the beginning, a quite different characterization has also been true: *Christmas is for workers*.

I'm not sure when I first realized this, but there's one early image that stands out in my mind. It's a scene that many people today won't even recognize, from an era when most homes were heated by a coal furnace. I remember a day just before Christmas, when my little-boy mind was completely wrapped up in the modest pile of presents under the Christmas tree and the special treats Mother was preparing in the kitchen. She was interrupting her work regularly to worry about whether the coal men would come. We didn't have enough coal in the bin to last through the next day, and in an Iowa winter, that was a grim prospect.

Suddenly, there was a grinding of gears from behind the house, a pounding open of our basement window, and then the sound of coal cascading down a metal chute into the coal room. (I didn't think that there could be a more comforting sound in the world than the sound of coal thundering into the basement on a cold winter's day!) Then the coal-begrimed driver came to the door to collect for delivery, and my childish mind was suddenly struck by a melancholy but mature thought: While I was excitedly waiting for Christmas, these coal-truck men were working so that other people could keep warm.

Just a few years later, I moved into the same workaday world. During holiday seasons, I worked as a "hopper" on a laundry and dry-cleaning delivery truck. I remember the twilight settling in on one Christmas Eve, and I also remember my anxiety to get home. But the driver of the laundry truck said, "These folks have to have their clothes tonight, before Christmas Day." And I can still remember the expressions of grateful relief as I delivered a suit here and a package of shirts there. I learned then that Christmas is for workers.

As I reminisce, the scenes are almost endless. I think of a Christmas Eve on board a train that was running several hours late. One of the trainmen apologized. "We're running with a short crew tonight. So many of our people call in sick on Christmas Eve." I sympathized with those who yielded to such a temptation, but I was grateful for the railroad personnel who knew that Christmas was for workers. I think of those hundreds of thousands of store clerks who have their most trying days of the year in the week before Christmas, and those millions of homemakers who fill every spare moment trying to put together some occasions of taste and beauty for the Christmas benefit of others. On the day after Christmas, many sit down in relief and exhaustion. Christmas certainly is for workers.

And *of course* it is! After all, the first Christmas announcement didn't come to a party at the Bethlehem Hilton, but to a group of workers out on the hillside. "And there were in the same country shepherds," the ancient, honored words declare, "abiding in the field, keeping watch over their flock by night" (Luke 2:8 KJV). Those shepherds were working— and the *night* shift, at that! But these shepherds also worked the day shift, and the swing shift as well; this was the nature of their job. Nevertheless, the night was special. There was a quietness about it, yet the shepherds had to keep their senses sharper than ever to prevent some wild animal or thief from carrying off a lamb in the darkness. Yes, the night had its own perils and responsibilities.

Let me pause here to make the picture clearer. Not only were the shepherds workers, they were among the most *despised* of workers. We like to say that all honest work is honorable, but some kinds of work don't bring invitations to join the country club. Shepherding was like that in Israel in the first century. Because of the nature of their work, shepherds couldn't keep the ceremonial laws that "good" people kept. They were seen as outsiders, living on the edge of town. And if anyone suffered a theft, the shepherds were the first to be suspected. Shepherding was lonely work, isolating its people from the general course of life and sometimes even from family life. If you were a first-century Jew, you might sentimentally recall that God had called a shepherd boy, David, to be Israel's favorite king. Yet, even so, you wouldn't want your daughter or your sister marrying a shepherd.

But let's get back to the shepherds who were working near Bethlehem that Christmas night. It was chilly; nights are cool in that semi-arid hill country. The sheep were sleeping most of the time, but the shepherds had to stay ready and alert to ensure their safety. These shepherds were rugged men: feet accustomed to picking their way through briers and stones; arms and hands sufficiently toned to sling a stone that would drive off a scavenger, yet gentle enough to help deliver a lamb; shoulders brawny enough to carry an injured sheep or to wrestle an attacking wild beast. The shepherds' hands were dirty from their work; their faces coarse from living outdoors; their bodies smelling of animals, dust, and perspiration. They were workers, and they were working hard, and Christmas came to them right where they were—at work.

Don't be surprised that Christmas came to people on the job. I can't think of one instance in the Scriptures when God called someone who was loafing. Moses saw the burning bush while he was out on a hillside, herding sheep. Samuel had to call young David in from tending sheep in the fields in order to crown him king. Nehemiah was working as a servant in a king's palace when he was called by God to go back to Jerusalem and help rebuild the city. Amos the prophet has given us some of the most moving exhortations in all of literature, but when interrogated by a representative of the king, he said, "I am no prophet, nor a prophet's son; but I am a herdsman, and a dresser of sycamore trees" (Amos 7:14).

So it is that some workers hurried into the birthplace of the Messiah that first Christmas night. They didn't have time to change clothes for the occasion; come to think of it, they probably didn't have other clothes into which they could change. The smell of their work was still on them, the dirt of the fields in the lines of their hands and faces. It wasn't hard for them to kneel before the manger; they knelt scores of times each day to tend their animals. The crudeness of the place where our Lord was born didn't seem out of place to them; most of the life they knew was crude, bare, and raw.

The Bible tells us nothing about the later life of the shepherds. Their story concludes with the words, "The shepherds returned, glorifying and praising God for all they had heard and seen, as it had been told them" (Luke 2:20). *The shepherds returned:* I expect that means they went right back to the fields and flocks from which they had come. As far as we know, they continued being shepherds until the day they died. I'm confident that they were *different* shepherds from that time forward. I don't think they ever forgot what happened that night, and I'm sure that they lived their lives in some marked fashion because of what they had experienced.

But I think they went on being shepherds. Not everyone is supposed to become a preacher. The Lord calls most of us to be workers in other places—kitchens, offices, executive suites, factories, stores, restaurants, classrooms, a delivery or sales route. And Christmas comes to all of these places. It comes to workers who are doing their thing, provided they are attentive to the angel song.

Thirty years later, Jesus gave special glory to work. "My Father is still working, and I also am working," he said (John 5:17). God is a worker. God has an unfathomable universe to keep in order, so God is always at work. Thus Jesus said, "Since the Father keeps working, an obligation is on me to work, as well."

What kind of work did Jesus do? As you follow him through the days of his ministry, you see him teaching the multitudes, healing the sick, blessing children, casting out demons, and listening to and talking with those who were generally scorned by society. The Bible says, on repeated occasions, that Jesus was "moved with compassion" as he saw the needs of those around him. In all of this he fulfilled the prophecy of Isaiah: "Surely he has borne our infirmities and carried our diseases" (Isaiah 53:4).

I have watched, and sometimes been part of, many kinds of hard labor. I have worked with men carrying great loads on a railroad loading dock. I have stood with women in the heat of an Iowa August as they perspired over a laundry mangle through long days. I have watched a teacher laboring week after week to educate and enlighten her class of young children, and I have seen nurses and their aides hurrying through the night hours with medicine trays and mercy. And, yes, I have boarded the inter-urban trains at 6:00 or 6:30 in the evening, along with executives and attorneys carrying attaché cases that meant more work for them at home that night. Indeed, work has many faces in our world.

But I think there is no harder labor than that which our Lord bore, and which he enjoins on us: to bear the grief and sorrows of other people. See Jesus in the midst of lepers, those who are blind, and those who are lame: Others hurry by, avoiding the sight, but Jesus gets under the weight— sometimes healing and sometimes prevented from healing by others' unbelief, but always loving. See him surrounded by lives that have been cheapened by sin: Jesus does not indulge in the luxury of condemning or of superior isolation. Instead, he picks up the load, the violence, the pain of their distraught and sinful lives.

No wonder, then, that the lonely, the disinherited, and the unwanted came to Jesus, and that having been near him, they walked away with lighter feet. But after they have gone, *he* walks on with bent form, for now he carries their grief and their sorrows. "My Father is always working, and I too must work."

The first Christmas came to workers. At first thought, this seems very remarkable, because our idea of Christmas is so much a matter of celebration and fun and reunion. But further thought says that this is just right. *Of course* Christmas would come to workers! Christmas means that God himself came to our world in Jesus Christ because there was work to be done. All of the world's inhabitants were heavy-laden, some with the heartbreak of life, some with counterfeit pleasures, and some with the sheer burden of living. So Jesus came to enter into the perspiration of life, to pull and strain at humanity's load.

And since Jesus came to do the hardest of all work—carrying humanity's grief, sorrow, and sin—how better can we celebrate Christmas than to become workers? Some four hundred years ago, Martin Luther chided a congregation: "There are many of you in this congregation who think to yourselves: 'If only I had been there! How quick I would have been to help the baby! I would have washed his linen.'...If you had been there at that time you would have done no better than the people of Bethlehem....Why don't you do it now? You have Christ in your neighbor. You ought to serve him, for what you do to your neighbor in need you do to the Lord Christ himself" (Roland Bainton, *The Martin Luther Christmas Book* [Fortress Press, 1948]).

If you want a great Christmas celebration this year, enter into the spirit of the One who came to our world to work at human burdens and who calls us to do the same. Look today and tomorrow and every day for the burdened, the lonely, the forgotten, the heavy-laden. Take on some burden you could so easily avoid, some problem that is not yours. Relieve someone's pain by drawing a little of it into yourself. Place food on some table, mercy in some life.

And as you do so, in simple human love and Christian faith, Christmas will come upon you all unbidden. It may be as bright as an angel song or as unpretentious as a sleeping flock, but it will come, because Christmas is for workers. God is working in this world, and we must work too.

11
Christmas Is for Spendthrifts

based on Matthew 2:1-12

Isn't it strange that Christmas giving has gotten a bad name? It has, you know. Mind you, the stores are filled with shoppers. Almost every year, business experts predict that we will have a high-spending, near-record-breaking year.

But shopping is accompanied by a good deal of muttering. Some shoppers are resolving (as they did last year, and the year before) that this will be the last time they'll spend so much money on presents. "Next year I'm cutting back on my list!" they say, or "I'm getting *out* of this Christmas rat race!" Others make a somewhat philosophical case: "Materialism has ruined Christmas. It's supposed to be a spiritual experience, but all of this commercialism has made it the most materialistic of all holidays." Still others take a sentimental turn: "I'd like to have an old-fashioned Christmas," they say, "where we give practical things—stockings, sweaters, gloves, underwear, homemade candy, preserves..."

No one can deny that Christmas has become very commercial. This reflects our human nature, in both its glory and its greed. Our minds see the potential in nearly every circumstance (and that's a *good* thing!), and then we easily get carried away with an insatiable appetite for more (and this is a *bad* thing). I'm afraid that the specialty catalogs that flood the mail in November testify to a tragic fact: Great numbers of us are buying presents for people who don't really need anything, so we struggle for something novel or bizarre that we hope will catch a person's fancy for a day or two. Yet it is both strange and sad that Christmas giving is getting a bad name, because if any part of our Christmas celebration has authentic roots in the original Christmas story, it is the act of *giving*.

I'm sure you remember the original occasion. At the time of Jesus' birth, some scholars in the Eastern world had concluded—partly from their study of the planets and, no doubt, partly from divine insight—that a new King of the Jews was to be born. These wise men then found their way to Bethlehem, where they bowed in worship before the baby Jesus; and in their adoration, they presented gifts to him: gold, frankincense, and myrrh. Incidentally, we always speak of the *three* wise men, but at no point does the Bible tell us how many there were; we assume their number on the basis of the three gifts. In any event, it is in the gifts of these wise men that the human side of the tradition of Christmas giving was first established.

When we decry the materialism of Christmas giving, we should remember that these first Christmas gifts were highly materialistic. They were items from the first-century equivalent of an exclusive shop. When we complain about the rat race of Christmas shopping, perhaps we should ponder the wise men. Did they go on a frantic shopping spree before they set out on their journey? Did they ask themselves, their spouses, and their respected counselors, "What do you think we should buy for the new king?" Did they ramble for hours through the bazaars and shops of some exotic Eastern city, rejecting one possibility after another, until at last they settled on gold, frankincense, and myrrh?

And what was it like when the wise men returned home? How did they tell their families or their scholarly colleagues about their experience? It was easy enough, of course, to speak of the wonder of the star, of their conversations with the scribes in Jerusalem, and of the unexpected climax to their journey at an exceedingly humble setting in Bethlehem. Perhaps they confessed the surprise they felt when they saw the peasant girl and the workman who was her husband. No, the scene they had encountered wasn't at all what they had expected for a new king.

I imagine someone interrupting the wise men's account of their journey: "You say the mother is a peasant girl, and the man with her a village carpenter? And they're staying in some stable in the backstreets of Bethlehem? And you gave the child gold, frankincense, and *myrrh?* You gave this poor little Jewish infant all those expensive things? What in the world made you *do* that?" And I imagine the wise men answering, sheepishly, "Well, it *seemed* the right thing to do...." Christmas, you see, is for *spendthrifts*. And the giving it inspires often defies logic.

Let's change the scene. Imagine Mary talking with some kind, Jewish peasant woman who has come by to see the new baby that was born in the stable behind the inn. Mary tells the woman of the astonishing visit by the wise men, then shows what the wise men brought: gold, frankincense, and myrrh. The peasant woman looks at the poor surroundings in which Mary is living, casts a critical eye over Mary's crude garments and the poor swaddling cloths in which the baby is wrapped, and shakes her head as she says, "They gave you these expensive knickknacks? What use is a gold medallion and imported perfume to an infant? Better they should have given you a dozen new diapers. *That,* you could have used."

But Christmas, you see, is for spendthrifts. It inspires people to do things that are sometimes extravagant, sometimes illogical, perhaps even irresponsible. Many years ago, the late Halford Luccock wrote a column in praise of the English carol "A Partridge in a Pear Tree."

> A partridge in a pear tree—what on earth could one do with that? That's the beauty of it! That makes it something to sing about! And folks have been singing about it for several hundred years. Would they have sung about a floor mop...or a teakettle or a foot warmer? Not much! (Luccock, *Like a Mighty Army*, Oxford University Press, 1954)

Dr. Luccock's attitude may trouble some of us. Yes, there is hunger in the world; yes, people need shelter, clothing, and medicine; and God knows we ought to be doing much more about such needs. And some of us remember childhood Christmas gifts of stockings, mufflers, and underclothes that were badly needed, and which we now look back on with much more sentiment than we felt at that time! Yes, there's much to be said for practical gifts. And yet, there's something about Christmas that ought to make us go a step beyond necessity and practicality. There ought to be something of the mood of gold, frankincense, and myrrh, even if we have to do our shopping at the local discount outlet.

Isn't that the philosophy behind our gift wrapping? Mind you, I'm a paper saver; I try to smuggle away the smooth portions of all those expensive papers so I can reuse them on smaller presents at some other time. But I'm glad for the glamour wrapping, illogical though it may be. That's also the way it works with such very practical gifts as fruit baskets and cheese delicacies. The fruit comes not in a paper bag, nor the cheese in butcher paper, but both with frills and color and bows and design. "Phony!" some Scrooge might say. "Like gold, frankincense, and myrrh," I want to reply.

And so, too, with our homemade products of the season. The cookies are cut and designed, and candies are the kind you make only once a year, the desserts have a distinctive holiday flavor, and the settings for meals somehow have that extra-special Christmas flair. Christmas not only means giving, it means giving with a flourish! The wise men set the pattern for this two millennia ago.

Ultimately, the most special quality of Christmas giving is *love*. Christmas giving that is done purely for business reasons, with no real affection or regard for the recipient, violates the Christmas spirit. So does the kind of giving that tries to impress or outdo others. And it's very sad, of course, when people give resentfully or bitterly, just as it's sad when people give without thought, simply settling on the first thing they see. But the fact that some maltreat and misuse Christmas giving is no reason to abandon it. On the contrary, we should *redeem* it! Let's return to the spirit of the first Christmas, when wise men shopped carefully to find just the right gift for a new king, then brought their wonderfully unlikely gifts to a poor baby in Bethlehem.

But let's go even further back in the story of giving. The tradition of Christmas giving is older and more profound than the wise men. The Gospel of John tells us where Christmas giving began, in words so familiar that we forget they describe the Christmas spirit: "For God so loved the world, that he gave his only begotten Son, that whosoever believeth in him should not perish, but have everlasting life" (John 3:16 KJV). Christmas giving began with God.

And have no doubt about it: God was a spendthrift! There was an irrational abandon in God's giving. Logic would say there must have been an easier way to reach and redeem the human soul, a gift less dramatic and less costly. But God gave his Son.

Do you suppose there was some celestial advisor of a penurious nature who questioned God's act? Did some keeper of the Heavenly Exchequer raise some altogether logical issues: "You have so many planets, and only one Son; why give him to planet Earth? And remember, Lord, how poor a record this Earth crowd has. These are the folks who gave you Sodom and Gomorrah. They make slaves of their fellow creatures and waste their natural resources. They hardly deserve a gift of any kind, when you've already given them so much and they've used it so poorly. And most of all, they should not be given *your Son*. This gift is well beyond the capacity and deservedness of these recipients."

If there had been such a celestial advisor, he or she would have been quite correct. When God gave his only begotten Son, he was a spendthrift. He was absurdly, irrationally generous. There is no logic that can justify such a gift.

But let's imagine, once again, the point of view of some of those recipients of God's gift. Imagine a meeting of philosophers and statesmen, hard at work on the problems of their first-century world. A religious enthusiast—one of the wise men, we imagine—breaks into their meeting with a message that he feels will answer all of their concerns: "Good news! God has sent the answer to our human problems—and it is a *gift*, at that!"

"What *sort* of gift?" the philosophers and leaders ask. "A world court, perhaps, or a structural plan for peace? Could this gift be some cure that will rid us of famines and plagues?"

And the wise man, his enthusiasm still fresh and undiminished, answers, "No, no: a *baby*. A little baby, born to a young Jewish couple over in Bethlehem of Judea. *He* is God's gift to our human race."

Surely we'd hear the philosophers and leaders mutter, "A *baby?* How *peculiar* of God! We need so many practical things, and God sends another baby. We have enough babies; it's *solutions* we need." George MacDonald captured the beauty and simplicity of God's precious gift in these simple, memorable words:

> They all were looking for a king
> To slay their foes and lift them high;
> Thou cam'st, a little baby thing
> That made a woman cry.
>
> ("That Holy Thing")

Jesus wasn't the gift the philosophers and tough-minded rulers wanted. But he was, and is, the gift we human beings need most. He is the priceless gift, God's saving Son. He is the gift of ultimate love, the gift that saves those who believe in him.

As I said at the outset, I'm sorry Christmas giving has gotten a bad name in recent years. The giving we do is all to the good if it comes from love. True, some abuse the spirit of giving, some exploit it, and some give thoughtlessly. No matter; giving is *good.* It brings out the best in us when we let it. And it is at the very heart of Christmas.

The wise men gave us the human example, with their fanciful, almost absurd gifts for a peasant baby. But, far more significant, God set the pattern. God, not caring how undeserving the recipients were, gave the only truly priceless gift in the universe, and gave in love. God was a spendthrift; and Christmas—still—is for all loving spendthrifts.

Give, and be glad.

12
Christmas Is
for Saints

ased on Luke 2:25-38

I have saved for last the theme I feared would appeal to you least. We all have some natural empathy for lonely people, workers, and even spendthrifts. But *saints?* Well, we just don't relate to the term. It's no wonder that the eve of All Saints Day has deteriorated into the completely secular Halloween, because saints don't easily fit into the icon of our daily lives.

It is also no wonder that the role of the saints in our Christmas story rarely gets the attention it deserves. The New Testament gives a bit more space to the story of two saints at Christmastime, Simeon and Anna, than it does to either the shepherds or the wise men. But since then, not many have noticed them. If they're mentioned at all, it's as an afterthought. And the fact that these two saints are both elderly hasn't enhanced their popularity. We sing so many carols about the wise men, the shepherds, and the angels, but to my knowledge only one reasonably popular

Christmas song gives a verse to the saints—James Montgomery's lyrics in "Angels from the Realms of Glory":

> Saints, before the altar bending,
> Watching long in hope and fear;
> Suddenly the Lord, descending,
> In his temple shall appear:
> Come and worship, come and worship,
> Worship Christ, the newborn King.

Novelists, playwrights, and composers haven't done much better by the saints. You've read and heard all kinds of fanciful, imaginative stories about the innkeeper, the shepherds, the wise men, the villagers, the donkeys, the sheep, the fireflies, and the flowers of the Christmas season; but how many stories or plays have you heard about Simeon and Anna? The American-English poet T. S. Eliot went inside Simeon's mind for a moving, sensitive poetic interpretation, but his poem is on a rather sophisticated level. I don't know if anyone has ever created a popular work around the saints of the Christmas story. It's pretty clear that Simeon and Anna will never seriously compete with Rudolph the Red-nosed Reindeer. Saints somehow aren't that marketable. Not often, at any rate.

But come to think of it, saints are the most *likely* participants in the Christmas story. They are the predictable part of a story that is otherwise chock-full of incongruities. We don't expect Jesus to be born in a manger behind an inn, and we don't expect hillside shepherds or wise men to make a pilgrimage to celebrate his birth. But since Jesus came to fulfill a divine promise and an ancient human longing, we *can* reasonably expect *saints* to be part of the story. *They* should be the ones most prepared in both mind and spirit to celebrate Jesus' coming, so *surely* they would be part of the event.

And they were. Simeon and Anna were there.

Let me tell you about these saints. Simeon, as I alluded to above, was apparently an older man. We don't know his exact age, but he was old enough to have been given assurance that he would not die until he had seen the Messiah. T. S. Eliot imagines Simeon saying, "My life is light, waiting for the death wind" ("A Song for Simeon," *The Complete Poems and Plays, 1909–1950,* Harcourt, Brace and Company, 1952). But more important than Simeon's age is that he was, according to the Scriptures, a good and pious man. Anna was also elderly, and while the writer of Luke's Gospel does not mention Simeon's age, we are told that Anna was eighty-four years old. She had been a widow for many years, and she was in the temple day after day, year after year, worshiping there "with fasting and prayer night and day" (Luke 2:37).

The law of the Jews required parents to have their boy babies circumcised at a given time and then bring the new baby to the temple for an act of purification. Joseph and Mary made their appointed pilgrimage expecting, I'm sure, that it would be a quiet, family affair. It is reasonable to believe that no one in Jerusalem knew them. They were an unpretentious peasant couple. The girl was pretty, no doubt, with the combination of her youth and her excitement of parenthood, and the young man was probably handsome in his sturdiness and in his attentiveness to his wife and child. But there would have been no unique, compelling reason to notice them.

Yet, attention came their way. First, from Simeon, awesome not only for his age and bearing, but because he was so profoundly moved by the sight of the little family. He took the baby Jesus in his arms and began to thank God, saying,

"Master, now you are dismissing your servant in peace,
    according to your word;
for my eyes have seen your salvation,

115

which you have prepared in the presence of all peoples,
a light for revelation to the Gentiles
and for glory to your people Israel." (Luke 2:29-32)

Joseph and Mary marveled at what was happening. Then
Simeon blessed them and spoke a special word of warning
to Mary. Then, we are told, Anna came to them. She was a
prophet, and when she saw the baby, she, like Simeon,
gave thanks to God and began to "speak about the child to
all who were looking for the redemption of Jerusalem"
(Luke 2:38). Considering the description of Anna's audience, perhaps we can say that she was spreading the good
news to a number of other saints, anonymous saints—people, that is, who were waiting for God's purposes to be fulfilled.

Perhaps you feel that this story of Simeon and Anna isn't
really part of the Christmas scene, since it took place several
days after the birth of Jesus. In truth, however, it must have
preceded the visit of the wise men, because we read that
immediately after their visit, the Holy Family fled to Egypt.
Perhaps any such uneasiness about these post-birth events
reflects our typical American celebrations. We make much of
the several weeks before Christmas as a setting for various
celebrations, both secular and religious, but then we tend to
direct our attention to the new year. In many other parts of
the world, the Christmas observance begins on Christmas
Day and then continues for the next twelve days, climaxing
on January 6, the day that for centuries has been celebrated
as the time when the wise men came to visit Jesus. So
Simeon and Anna are very much a part of the Christmas
story, as Luke's Gospel indicates.

Perhaps the reason we so easily ignore Simeon and Anna
is because their appearance on the Christmas scene was not
so glamorous. They weren't summoned by an angel on a
hillside, nor did they follow a beckoning star. In fact, their
situation was not at all exciting. For years they had waited

116

and prepared themselves for such a time as this, and when at last it came, they were ready to receive it.

But in a thoughtful measure of the matter, most of us might feel closer to Simeon and Anna than to the shepherds or the wise men. It's not that we are so saintly, but rather that our lives are generally inclined to a more predictable religious experience. In a sense, the several participants in the Christmas story symbolize the various kinds of conversion to Christianity. The shepherds are like the dramatic conversions: people saved from alcoholism and gambling, or like Saul of Tarsus, struck by a dramatic revelation. The wise men are like those persons who follow an intellectual search: They look—perhaps for years—at the evidence and the problems, for a while almost lose their way, then experience that special kind of intuition that leads them at last to the reality of Jesus Christ. Simeon and Anna, however, are like that great body of persons who live earnest, generally good lives (though the two of them lived with more impressive devotion than most of *us* would claim) until one day they are led to the fullness of Jesus Christ.

In a sense, Simeon and Anna had spent years preparing themselves for just this experience. And when it came, it was deeply moving, but it was not by any means so dramatic as an angel visitor on the hillside, or a star shining compellingly in the sky. Perhaps you have come to your faith in just such a predictable way.

As I see it, the most impressive part of the story of Simeon and Anna is that *they waited*. Does this sound altogether uninspiring? Frankly, it is. But it strikes me that saints do *a lot* of waiting. Others grow impatient with causes and with people, but saints keep on waiting.

Several years ago, a secular writer analyzed what was happening in the slums and ghettos of a major city. It was during a time of renewed social consciousness, especially on the part of the young. The writer said that urban dwellers in the area had gotten cynical about it all. They had seen bright young men and women (and some middle-aged ones, too) come into the neighborhood each year full of enthusiasm and promises of social revolution. After a few months—or, at most, a year—they'd be gone, and a new crew would come in. These bright visionaries had plenty of enthusiasm and exciting ideas but no staying power. By contrast, the writer noted, some priests, nuns, and mission workers—both black and white, Catholic and Protestant—kept on working in the area year after year after year. These persons came without fanfare or glamour, but they stayed. Saints do a lot of waiting.

The same can surely be said about our dealings with individuals. Most of us are humane enough to give a pat on the back, to speak a helpful word, or to encourage a person after a failure or two. But the saints are those who keep on believing and waiting.

One woman in California tells such a story. She volunteered at a nursing home to visit someone who had no other visitors, and she was led to Agnes, an older woman who was not especially attractive. When the visitor offered to read from the Bible, Agnes asked, "Oh, is it Christmastime already?" When told that it was not, Agnes explained that a lot of people always came to read the Bible at Christmastime. "Then they go away," she said, "saying they'll come back, but they never do. I thought you must be one of those church people."

Now the visitor knew she would *have* to return, though the setting was far from appealing. And she *did* return. She came regularly and often, and she even began bringing her family. One day it was clear that Agnes would soon die. Agnes testified that she had become a Christian because of the things the visitor and her family had done. "How, Agnes?" the visitor asked. "How did we show you?" And Agnes answered, simply, "You came back" (Linda Schiwitz, "The Reluctant Visitor," *Guideposts,* April 1979). Saints do a lot of waiting.

Obviously, it isn't *idle* waiting. Indeed, waiting is often very hard work. It is not only that routine tasks themselves become tedious, but also that it is so difficult to keep faith. When we read that Anna was in the temple day and night at eighty-four years of age, that she fasted and prayed, we see a stalwart example of a saint who is *waiting*. Lesser souls rise with enthusiasm and fall off as time goes by, but the great souls keep on waiting, believing, expecting. Simeon, Luke tells us, had been "looking forward to the consolation of Israel" (Luke 2:25); and because Simeon waited so earnestly, God revealed that he would not die until he had seen the Messiah. Did Simeon sometimes say to God, "Have you forgotten? Have you noticed, perhaps, that I'm getting older?" Regardless, he kept on waiting; saints are very good at waiting.

Why is this so? It is because saints are fed by *hope*. Normal excitement wanes as quickly as it rises, but hope has inner resources by which it is renewed. When the wind blows fiercely or the path grows steep, others lose heart. But the saints keep on hoping, keep on waiting.

Have you noticed how hope rises in a special way during the Christmas season? As surely as people treat one another with more love and are more ready to wish one another well at this time of the year, so too do we get new hope at this season. Prospects may be as dim or foreboding as ever, but Christmas awakens hope.

Indeed, the spirit of hope seems to overflow upon even the secular souls who decry Christmas. In the words of James Montgomery,

> Saints, before the altar bending,
> *Watching long in hope and fear;*
> Suddenly the Lord, descending,
> In his temple shall appear.
> ("Angels from the Realms of
> Glory," emphasis added)

At this season, hope comes anew to all; and with this hope we rise to meet the disheartening and the impossible.

But the saints carry this spirit with them all through the year. They keep watching, waiting, hoping. They believe in God and in Christ, and because of their believing, they will not give up. And because they wait and wait, Christmas comes to them. Not so dramatically, perhaps, as to the shepherds or the wise men. But it comes, and it stays. Indeed, the coming of Christmas the *saints* experience may be the best of all!

Come, then, to join the saints who work and wait because they hope. Join those who, because they believe in the promise of God, will not allow themselves to be lost in despair.

REFLECTION

Nell W. Mohney

*ow the L*ORD *had said unto Abram,
Get thee out of thy country...unto a land that I
will shew thee.*
                                                    —Genesis 12:1 KJV

Among the things we need to take with us on our Christmas journey is the wonderful gift of memory. At whatever age or place you find yourself now, you can be instantly transported to a time when you were five or six and remember a special Christmas experience. Or you can remember what your world looked like when you were just sixteen, or recall the events of your wedding day.

Let us use this gift to remember how God began the trip to Bethlehem. God needed a nation of people who would know the one true God and understand God's purpose for the world. God chose Abram, a seventy-five-year-old man living in Haran. Scholars tell us that Haran was a well developed and civilized land where people of wealth had beautiful homes made of stone and cedar. Imagine a man of retirement age, with a wife who was sixty-five, being asked to leave his comfortable life and live the remainder of his

121

years in a tent in a strange land. The miracle is that Abram heard and heeded God's call and became a blessing to all future generations.

I am convinced that Abram heard God's call because he took time for silence and listening. His life was not over-stuffed and cluttered with busyness, hurry, and stress.

What about you? Will you take time in silence to remember God's blessings in your life? Will you be quiet enough to hear God directing you toward an act of service or an errand of love? God may be calling you to spend time reading to a toddler or listening to a teenager or encouraging a spouse or visiting a shut-in or doing other errands of love. Let us, like Abram, hear and heed God's call.

PART FOUR

Come Home for Christmas

James A. Harnish

INTRODUCTION

The people who came to worship on that particular Sunday never expected my sermon to begin with the sound of Bing Crosby singing "I'll Be Home for Christmas." Although it took them by surprise, the response from the World War II generation—many with tears in their eyes—confirmed my expectation that the sound of Crosby's voice singing that song would touch a deep place in their souls. Former soldiers shared their memories of hearing that tune on a troop ship crossing the Atlantic, in a snowbound Army base in Europe, and on a sun-soaked airstrip in the Pacific. One remembered sitting alone in a Manhattan movie theater watching Crosby and Fred Astaire in *Holiday Inn* (in which Bing movingly performed another of the best-loved Christmas songs of all time, "White Christmas"). Spouses and parents remembered hearing "I'll Be Home for Christmas" on the radio as they sat down to Christmas dinner with an empty chair at the table. Crosby's silky rendition brought back all the feelings of a time when the only thing they really wanted for Christmas was the one thing they could not have, namely, to be together and to be at home.

The picture of being home for Christmas touches a soul-level longing within just about every one of us in every generation. The Christmas season may intensify it, but the feeling is timeless. It's like Scarlett dragging herself back to

Tara, Dorothy trying to get back to Kansas, George Bailey discovering that it really is a wonderful life, ET phoning home, or Tom Hanks as plane crash survivor Chuck Noland, sitting alone on the shore of the remote tropical island and gazing longingly across the waters of the deep blue sea. These famous movie images reflect a common reality: that we all share a basic, human longing for a place to call home.

And this soul-level longing for home is a primary biblical metaphor for something even deeper, something even more timeless: the universal human longing for an intimate relationship with God. We follow it with the people of Israel, wandering through the wilderness in search of the Promised Land. We hear it in the pained, mournful songs of exiles in Babylon, hoping to one day return to Jerusalem. We see it in Mary and Joseph, going up to Bethlehem to register with the census, searching for a private corner in which their baby could be born. We identify with it in Jesus' parable of the runaway son who returns to his father. We taste it around the Passover table with Jesus' promise that in his Father's house there are many rooms. We stand in awe before it when Jesus promises the thief on the cross a place in paradise. We anticipate it in John's Technicolor visions of the new Jerusalem, coming down out of heaven with a shout,

> See, the home of God is among mortals.
> He will dwell with them;
> they will be his peoples,
> and God himself will be with them. (Revelation 21:3)

The truth about every one of us is that we are lost—homesick—runaway children who long to come home to God. Noted British author and poet G. K. Chesterton captured the sense of this universal longing in his classic poem "The House of Christmas." Here is just a part of what he wrote:

> To an open house in the evening
>   Home shall men come,
> To an older place than Eden
>   And a taller town than Rome;
> To the end of the way of the wandering star,
> To the things that cannot be and that are,
> To the place where God was homeless
>   And all men are at home.
>   (from *Modern British Poetry,* pages 210-11)

Chesterton used the word *men* the way we would say *all* or *humankind,* yet he has described the most profound reality that applies to each and every one of us: We are created for a living, loving, growing relationship with God. Nothing else—regardless of how much we pay for it or how much of ourselves we give away to achieve it—can satisfy that hunger. Augustine got it right when he prayed, "Thou hast made us for Thyself and our souls are restless until they find their rest in Thee." During Christmastime, the gospel invites us to find our way home to God; to follow the path that leads to the manger of Bethlehem; to make our way "to the place where God was homeless" and all of us are at home.

My hope is that through these words, the living Word that became flesh in Jesus will become a tangible reality in the lives and relationships of the readers and that together, we will find our way home to the love of God, which was born among us at Bethlehem. German theologian Jürgen Moltmann described the process of discovery that I invite you to share:

> The coming One is in the process of his coming and can be grasped only in that light: as on the road, and walking with us.... The way of Christ comes into being under the feet of the person who walks it. To tread the way of Christ means believing in him. Believing in him means going with him along the part of the road he is taking at the present moment. (*The Way of Jesus Christ,* Fortress Press, 1993; pages 33-34).

13
Come Home
to Love

**ased on Jeremiah 33:1-16;
1 Thessalonians 2:17–3:13**

*For men are homesick in their homes,
    And strangers under the sun,
And they lay their heads in a foreign land
    Whenever the day is done.
Here we have battle and blazing eyes,
And chance and honor and high surprise;
But our homes are under miraculous skies
    Where the yule tale was begun.*
(G. K. Chesterton, "The House of Christmas,"
                in *Modern British Poetry*)

Have you ever been homesick? Tucked away in the attic
of my personality is a week at summer camp when I was a
twelve-year-old kid, exploding with hormones, acne, and
insecurity. I started having a toothache early in the week,
but like any red-blooded, adolescent boy, I wasn't about to

admit it to anyone. As the days went by, the tooth got worse. By the time I got home and to the dentist, it had developed into a full-blown, pus-filled abscess. I never faced the debilitating kind of homesickness I've seen in midadolescent campers since then, but I remember lying awake one night in the cabin with an ache in my tooth and a deeper ache in the pit of my soul. At that moment, I would have given anything just to be home!

My adolescent experience of homesickness is not worth comparing with the homesickness Dietrich Bonhoeffer experienced in 1943. While Bing Crosby was crooning "I'll Be Home for Christmas" for American soldiers, Bonhoeffer was writing Christmas letters from a Nazi prison cell. In those letters he confessed that there is nothing more painful than homesickness. He found that "nothing can make up for the absence of someone whom we love." He declared that there is no substitute for it. The only thing he could do was wait. He wrote, "We have to suffer unspeakably from the separation, and feel the longing till it almost makes us ill...for the gap, as long as it remains unfilled, preserves the bonds between us" (*Letters and Papers from Prison,* pages 167, 176).

There is a genuinely human sense in which every one of us is homesick. It is as common as baseball. When *Time* magazine named record-breaking hitter Mark McGwire as the 1998 "Hero of the Year," the writers quoted former Commissioner of Baseball A. Bartlett Giamatti, who said, "Baseball is about going home and how hard it is to get there and how driven is our need" (*Time,* December 28, 1998, page 139). And that need was never more driven, *Time* said, than it was during what was called "the political plague year" through which our nation had passed. We are driven by a deep, inner longing for home.

Feelings of homesickness permeate the scriptures. We feel this in the words of a homesick prophet named Jeremiah. Like Bonhoeffer, Jeremiah was in prison. He could see destruction coming: the city in ashes, the Temple sacked, homes destroyed, lives disrupted, and the people carried off into exile. But in spite of the obvious oppression and destruction, Jeremiah could see something else, something less obvious but no less real. The Spirit of God gave Jeremiah eyes to see what G. K. Chesterton referred to as "the things that cannot be [but] are." Jeremiah envisioned the hope that one day the Lord would gather up the exiles and bring them home. With prophetic imagination, he could see God's promise of healing, restoration, return, and renewal.

In this place of which you say, "It is a waste without human beings or animals," in the towns of Judah and the streets of Jerusalem that are desolate...there shall once more be heard the voice of mirth and the voice of gladness. (Jeremiah 33:10-11)

Jeremiah pictured a righteous branch growing out of the broken stump of David (ancestor of the broken, devastated tribes of Israel and Judah). Jeremiah saw God's promise of justice and righteousness being fulfilled. He could hear the laughter of homesick exiles dancing along the highway that would bring them home.

Like Bonhoeffer's Christmas letter from prison, Paul's letter to the Thessalonians also throbs with the pain of separation from people he loved. Eugene Peterson captured the emotion of Paul's pain in his paraphrase of 1 Thessalonians 2:17:

Do you have any idea how very homesick we became for you, dear friends? Even though it hadn't been that long and it was only our bodies that were separated from you, not our hearts, we tried our very best to get back to see you. You can't imagine how much we missed you! *(The Message)*

Because he could not be with them in person, Paul prayed for those he loved.

May God our Father himself and our Master Jesus clear the road to you! And may the Master pour on the love so it fills

131

your lives and splashes over on everyone around you, just as it does from us to you. (1 Thessalonians 3:11-12 *The Message*)

Some of us know the homesickness Paul described in terms of human relationships. We find ourselves at Christmastime with a huge, aching hole in the center of our souls because of the empty space that used to be filled by someone we loved. Death, divorce, disagreement, distance—whatever the cause, the empty chair at the table is the tangible witness of the relationship for which there is simply no substitute. All the signs, songs, and symbols of the Christmas season intensify the emptiness we feel. We share with the Hebrew exiles the full weight of separation from the people we love and the things in which we have placed our trust.

If the experience of homesickness is true in our human relationships, it is even more profoundly true in our relationship with God. When it comes down to it, our search for that soul-centering place where we know that we are at home with God is the deepest, strongest, most-powerful longing in our human existence. The Bible says that nothing can substitute for the presence of the God who loves us and whom we instinctively desire to love (e.g., Psalms 42:1-8; 143:6-8; Acts 17:26-28; Hebrews 11:13-16). The longing for God is planted so deeply within us that we can never escape it, though God knows we try. We run after all sorts of substitutes, but I know of only one pathway that will lead us home to the love of God. The only way I know to find the fullness of God's love in human experience and the hope and promise of new life for the future is to follow the well-worn path that leads to a baby in a manger. Watch him grow up in Mary and Joseph's home. Walk with him along the dusty roads of Palestine. Listen to his words. Feel his presence. Follow in obedience to his call. Suffer and die with him on the cross. Be raised to new life with him in the Resurrection. Come to know Jesus, and we will find the full expression of the love of God in human flesh. Follow him, and we will find our way home.

But how does it happen? How do we experience the love of God that is born among us in Bethlehem? When we tell the Nativity story, we tend to do it in Radio City Music Hall style, with soaring angels, thundering orchestras, and mass choirs singing the "Hallelujah!" chorus. But although this may be an appropriate way to celebrate the meaning Jesus' coming has in our lives, that's probably not the way the Nativity happened.

It happened, if we read the story straight, in an obscure village, among a crowd of poor, singularly unimportant refugees who were forced to return to their hometowns by the oppressive power of Roman occupation. It happened through a nondescript man and his pregnant wife who went to Bethlehem because it was the city of his ancestor David, and they were required to register with the census there. It happened in the dark corner of a cave that served as shelter for the animals. It happened silently, except for the sound of a woman in labor and the cry of a newborn child. It happened just the way it happens for every child born into the human race: "She [Mary] gave birth to her firstborn son" (Luke 2:7).

When the old Dutch master Brueghel painted the story, in *Numbering at Bethlehem*, he set the scene in a very ordinary Flemish village with a winter snow falling on all sorts of very ordinary people. In the foreground, a farmer is butchering a pig. From one corner, a woodsman carries in a load of firewood. Little Dutch children are cavorting on a frozen pond. A young man makes an obvious pass at a teasing young maid. In front of the village inn, a crowd has gathered around a bored-looking bureaucrat who haggles with a questioning taxpayer. It's all very ordinary. The only hint that there might be more going on here is a Christmas wreath that hangs over the inn door. It's enough to make us search the scene more closely. Finally, you find them. Down in the lower left corner of the canvas, inconspicuous in the crowd, a very ordinary young woman rides into this very ordinary town on the back of a very ordinary donkey, which is being led by a very ordinary, bearded peasant. The old Dutch master captured on his canvas the reality that Phillips Brooks described in his words to a familiar carol:

> How silently, how silently, the wondrous gift is given;
> So God imparts to human hearts the blessings of his heaven.
> No ear may hear his coming, but in this world of sin,
> Where meek souls will receive him, still the dear Christ enters
>   in.
>
> ("O Little Town of Bethlehem")

As I watch the way "ordinary" people experience the extraordinary love of God in Christ, I have increasingly less confidence in the loud, gaudy, noisy demonstrations of religious experience that masquerade for spiritual power. I try to focus instead on the quiet, ordinary ways in which the love of God becomes a reality in the lives of ordinary people who discipline themselves to see, feel, hear, and know the presence of Jesus in the ordinary places of their lives. In following Jesus, they find their way home to the love of God for which they so desperately seek. The journey begins when we learn to pray:

> O holy Child of Bethlehem, descend to us, we pray;
> Cast out our sin, and enter in, be born in us today.
> We hear the Christmas angels the great glad tidings tell;
> O come to us, abide with us, our Lord Emmanuel!
>
> ("O Little Town of Bethlehem")

14

Come Home to Hope

ased on Luke 1:26-66; Colossians 1:24-27

There fared a mother driven forth
Out of an inn to roam;
In the place where [God] was homeless
All men are at home.
The crazy stable close at hand,
With shaking timber and shifting sand,
Grew a stronger thing to abide and stand
Than the square stones of Rome.
(G. K. Chesterton, "The House of Christmas,"
in *Modern British Poetry*)

The highways are crowded and the airports are full. Everyone seems to be going somewhere for Christmas. One year at Christmastime, my wife, Marsha, and I flew to Birmingham, Alabama, for a wedding celebration. In the taxi on the way from the airport to the hotel, Marsha asked the driver if he was busy with all the Christmas travelers. "Not really," he said. "Our business falls off this time of year. People traveling for Christmas always have someone coming to meet them."

The driver made great sense. A business traveler needs a taxi, but Christmas travelers always have someone coming to meet them. We saw it in the eyes of a freshly scrubbed, closely cropped soldier who scanned the airport for the familiar faces of his parents. We could hear it in the laughter of grandparents who stepped off the jetway and wrapped their arms around a toddler with reindeer antlers on his head, complete with a little Christmas tree ball hanging from the antler. We could feel it in the anxious glances of children flying alone, scanning the airport for the single parent who waited to meet them. The hope within each Christmas traveler is that someone will be coming to meet them. And the hope in the soul of every "traveler" following that bright, shining star is that when we get to Bethlehem, someone will be there to meet us too.

Among the hopeful travelers along the highways of the Nativity story is a young woman—a girl, actually—named Mary. Her home was in Nazareth, but Luke says she "went with haste" to visit Elizabeth, her relative, up in the hill country of Judea.

Mary had good reason to get out of Nazareth. Engaged but not yet married to a man named Joseph, Mary, a virgin, had just confirmed that she was pregnant. She knew that the child was a gift from God, but she also knew that no one in Nazareth would believe it. She knew that Joseph had every reason to divorce her and throw her into the street. She knew of the Old Testament law that required that she be stoned to death. Mary had good reason to be running for her life.

Mary had reasons for running to her kinswoman, Elizabeth. Elizabeth was far too old to have a child. She had been barren all her life. But to everyone's surprise, the impossible had happened. She had conceived a child and was now six months into her pregnancy. Perhaps Elizabeth would understand the emotions Mary felt. Perhaps she would share the odd mixture of confusion and joy, doubt and faith, fear and hope that stirred within Mary's soul. Perhaps Elizabeth would understand the suspicious stares of the nosy neighbors of Nazareth. Perhaps she could identify with the embarrassed rejection by relatives and the vicious virtue of self-righteous religious leaders. Most of all, Elizabeth might actually believe that impossible things could become possible with God.

The Gospel story invites us to share the moment Mary walked through the door of Elizabeth's house. Mary called out to Elizabeth, and Luke records that "when Elizabeth heard Mary's greeting, the child leaped in her [Elizabeth's] womb" (1:41).

Reading through this story took me back to Christmas 1971. I was a full-time seminary student; my wife was teaching school and going to graduate school. We were so poor we used to tear paper napkins in half so they would last twice as long. (This didn't save much money, but it made us feel better!) That year we traveled to the hill country of Western Pennsylvania to celebrate Christmas with my relatives. Like Mary, we were pregnant with our firstborn child. I liked using that plural pronoun—*we* were pregnant—but Marsha kept reminding me that she felt the effects of the pregnancy somewhat more directly than I did!

To save money, Marsha had sewn her own maternity clothes. I remember one dress in particular. It was pink velour. (The 1970s were, after all, an era in fashion that many of us would be just as happy to forget!) We were seven months along, right about where Elizabeth was in this story. The baby, whom we would later name Carrie Lynn, showed every sign of being about as hyperactive as her father. We still laugh about the way that pink velour dress would shake all over like a bowlful of jelly every time the baby "leaped in her womb."

137

Nothing compares with the feeling of a baby kicking inside a mother's womb. It is a tangible sign of the promise of a new life. It is the visual expression of something that is not yet fulfilled but will one day be. It is the evidence of life to come. Elizabeth responded to the kick in her womb with a song of hope: "Blessed are you among women, and blessed is the fruit of your womb.... And blessed is she who believed that there would be a fulfillment of what was spoken to her by the Lord" (Luke 1:42, 45).

Elizabeth knew the meaning of hope. Biblical hope is the deep, inner certainty—just as real as a baby kicking in a mother's womb—that God will fulfill what God has spoken. Hope is the inner assurance that against all odds, and in spite of everything the world calls evidence, God's kingdom will come, and God's will shall be done on earth as it is in heaven. Hope is the often unseen guarantee that in spite of all the world's violence and hostility, one day the nations "shall beat their swords into plowshares, / and their spears into pruning hooks; / nation shall not lift up sword against nation, neither shall they learn war any more" (Micah 4:3). Hope is the gut-level confidence that, in spite of everything the world does to contradict it, one day "justice [will] roll down like waters, / and righteousness like an ever-flowing stream" (Amos 5:24). Hope is the deep, inner conviction that one day, "every knee should bend, / in heaven and on earth and under the earth, / and every tongue should confess / that Jesus Christ is Lord, / to the glory of God the Father" (Philippians 2:10-11). Hope is the deep, inner awareness— like the awareness of a woman who carries a child—that God's promises will one day be fulfilled. For Elizabeth and Mary, hope was the very personal realization that God's promise was being fulfilled in and through the flesh and blood of their very human, very ordinary lives.

It wasn't much of a sign—just a baby's kick in a woman's womb. But it was enough experiential evidence to become the sign of hope that God would fulfill God's promises. And in reality, it doesn't take a lot of what the world calls evidence to keep hope alive. It didn't take much of a sign for American writer Henry Wadsworth Longfellow; just the sound of a bell in a church steeple on Christmas Day. He described it in one of his best-known poems, "Christmas Bells."

> I heard the bells on Christmas Day
> Their old, familiar carols play,
>   And wild and sweet
>   The words repeat
> Of peace on earth, good-will to men!

The year was 1863. This nation was caught in the deadly grip of the Civil War. The prior year had seen the horrors of Gettysburg, the ghastliest, bloodiest, deadliest single event in the history of this country. The original version of the poem describes the awful reality of the war in lines that the Christmas card publishers always leave out and which soloists in Christmas shows on television never sing.

> Then from each black, accursed mouth
> The cannon thundered in the South,
>   And with the sound
>   The carols drowned
> Of peace on earth, good-will to men!

Imagining all the homes—from one end of the nation to the other—that would have an empty place at the table that Christmas, Longfellow went on:

> It was as if an earthquake rent
> The hearth-stones of a continent,
>   And made forlorn
>   The households born
> Of peace on earth, good-will to men!

No wonder Longfellow was tempted to doubt God's promise of peace:

> And in despair I bowed my head;
> "There is no peace on earth," I said;
>   "For hate is strong,
>   And mocks the song
> Of peace on earth, good-will to men!"

Then Longfellow heard a bell in a church steeple on Christmas Day. It wasn't much, but it was enough to give him hope.

> Then pealed the bells more loud and deep:
> "God is not dead; nor doth he sleep!
>   The Wrong shall fail,
>   The Right prevail,
> With peace on earth, good-will to men!"
> (from *The Complete Poetical Works of Longfellow,*
>   Houghton Mifflin, 1893; pages 289-90)

It wasn't much of a sign by the world's standards, but the ringing of the church bells was enough; it was enough to be the sign of hope, just like the child leaping in Elizabeth's womb.

Elizabeth never could have explained that event; there is no evidence that she ever tried. But she knew—from someplace so deep within her that she could never forget—that the child kicking in her womb was the sign of God's saving purpose being accomplished through her. The child was named John. We know him as John the Baptist, the one who prepared the way for the coming of the Lord.

Mary never could have explained the baby in her womb; there's no evidence that she ever tried. The New Testament doesn't attempt to analyze the scientific probability for the virgin birth. It was a mystery to be celebrated, not a thesis to be argued. By the world's standards, it was utterly incomprehensible. But Mary knew that the child in her womb was the hope of God's saving purpose being accomplished in human history. She knew that God's living Word was becoming flesh within her. She could feel the love of God becoming a tangible reality through her life.

The shepherds never could have explained it; there is no evidence that they ever tried. All they knew for sure was that in the darkness of the night they had received good news of a great joy that was coming for all people: "To you is born this day in the city of David a Savior, who is Christ the Lord. And this will be a sign for you: you will find a babe wrapped in swaddling cloths and lying in a manger" (Luke 2:11-12 RSV).

Those wise men, stargazers, mysterious visitors from the East never explained it. But they were wise enough to follow the beckoning Bethlehem star until it led them to the Christ Child, and they offered their best gifts in homage to the promise of this newborn king.

Joseph never could have explained it; there is no evidence in the New Testament that he ever tried. But he knew in a soul-level place, where knowing leads toward obedience, that this child was the sign of God's presence with us in human flesh. He obeyed the angel's command, even when obedience meant packing up his tiny family and hiding out as refugees in Egypt.

By the world's standards, there may not be much of a sign in our lives. We may never be able to fully or adequately explain or comprehend it. But like Elizabeth and Mary, we can feel the deep, inner hope that God is at work to accomplish God's loving purpose through us. Just as surely as Elizabeth felt the baby leaping in her womb, we can know that the very same love of God that became flesh within Mary's body is becoming a reality in this world through us. As shocking as it may sound, the amazing affirmation of Scripture is that in the same way the body of Jesus was being formed in the womb of Mary, the life of the living Christ can be formed within each of us. The sign of hope for every person of faith is simply this: "Christ in you, the hope of glory" (Colossians 1:27).

Reflecting on the way the sign was given to Mary, Bible scholar Robert Mulholland came to this conclusion:

> Every Christian is called to be a Mary. We are called to offer ourselves to God in such radical abandonment and availability that the Christ of God can be brought forth through our lives into the world. . . . Many desire this and actively offer to God disciplines of loving obedience through which Christ can be formed in them.
>
> (*The Upper Room Disciplines,* 1997, page 365)

The hope of every Christmas traveler is that someone will come to meet them. The One who meets us at Bethlehem is the living Christ, the One who becomes flesh in each of us.

15
Come Home
to Mercy

ased on Luke 1:68-79; 3:1-18; 15:11-32

A child in a foul stable,
*   Where the beasts feed and foam;*
Only where He was homeless
*   Are you and I at home;*
We have hands that fashion and heads that know,
But our hearts we lost—how long ago!
In a place no chart nor ship can show
*   Under the sky's dome.*
            (G. K. Chesterton, "The House of Christmas,"
                        in *Modern British Poetry*)

The invitation has gone out, and all our names are on it. The invitation this Christmas season is to come home in our relationship with God. Come, to paraphrase G. K. Chesterton, "to the place where God was homeless and all of us are at home."

The journey home begins with our deep awareness that

143

we are created for a living, loving, growing relationship with God, and that we will be restless wanderers until we come home. The journey leads us to that place where we name our hunger for the love of God to become a living reality in us, even as it became a living reality in the womb of Mary.

But if we tell the truth, the whole truth, and nothing but the truth, we know that's not the whole story. We know that we are not innocent, sweet, obedient little children who for some unknown reason happened to wander away from God. If we tell the whole truth, we know that we are rebellious children who have, in ways large and ways small, spurned the loving will of God. We are defiant children who have denied the claim of God's love on our lives. We are insolent children who have turned our backs and run away from home. We are all a little like G. K. Chesterton, who, habitually lost, once sent his wife a telegram: "Am at Market Harborough. Where ought I to be?" The one word answer came back: "Home." Chesterton's wife assumed that if she got him back home, it would be easier to get him going in the right direction.

One of the best-known stories Jesus ever told is a homecoming parable about a lost son who finds his way home. But the story doesn't begin with the son's return. The story begins with the ruthless, rebellious way he left home. He took his birthright, Jesus said, took everything his father had to give him, and ran away from home as fast as his insubordinate legs could carry him. Jesus said that he "squandered his wealth in wild living" (Luke 15:13 NIV). This runaway son followed his own way, and wasted his life in willful rebellion against the loving purpose for which he had been born.

My own story of rebellion has never been as colorful as the rebellion of the runaway son. I grew up as a "good boy." In the evangelical tradition in which I was raised, I heard dramatic testimonies of notorious sinners who repented and turned to God. Sometimes they made my life look so boringly good that I felt like doing some world-class sinning just so I would have a colorful story to tell. I remember searching and praying for a dramatic conversion experience like those described by other people. I guess I was more like the elder brother in Jesus' parable, the self-righteous goody two-shoes who never physically walked away from home, but who, in the bitterness of his heart, was just as far removed from the love of his father as his younger brother was when wallowing in the pig sty.

The Bible never flinches on telling the truth: "All we like sheep have gone astray; / we have all turned to our own way" (Isaiah 53:6). If we tell the whole truth of our lives, we can name the detours we have taken from the way of God's love. We know the intersections where we have chosen the path of self-interest rather than the way of self-giving love revealed in Jesus.

The Bible has a word for our running away from God. The Bible calls it *sin*. Because sin is such a universal part of our human experience, the liturgical road map for this time of year always leads us into the wilderness where we are confronted with John the Baptist. He's not an easy person to fit into our cultural Christmas traditions. I can't imagine him singing "Jingle Bells" or trimming a tree. He's not the kind of guest you invite for Christmas dinner. His message is not the kind of thing quoted in greeting cards. But the Gospel writers all agree that John is the one who came to prepare the way, to set things straight, to clear the road, to open up the highway for God. He comes like a spiritual bulldozer, pushing away the clutter and plowing through the trash that gets in the way of our coming to God and of God's coming to us. Luke records that John "went into all the region around the Jordan, proclaiming a baptism of repentance for the forgiveness of sins" (Luke 3:3).

To repent is to turn around and go in a new direction. Repentance means that I turn from the rebellious path of my sinful self-orientation and begin walking in the direction of God's self-giving love. John's call to repentance reminds us

145

that if what we read in the Christmas gospel and sing in the Christmas carols is true, it calls us to a radical transformation of human life. We're not talking about rearranging the furniture to make room for a Christmas tree. We're not talking about dusting off the surface of the table so that none of the Christmas guests will notice the dust underneath. We're talking about radical transformation that penetrates into the deepest part of our human personality and begins to shape and transform us into the likeness of God's love revealed in Jesus.

Beauty and the Beast is a classic tale of radical transformation. It's the story of an angry beast whose only hope of being transformed into a genuine human being is to be loved in his unlovable condition by a beautiful woman. At first, Beauty is frightened by the Beast's large stature, his meanness, his power. But over time, the unearned love of Beauty transforms the Beast into a man.

That's how Jesus comes to transform us. If we are honest, there is probably a part of us that prefers the Beast within us. There is something within us that prefers the devouring power that looks for all the world like strength; a sinful part of us that resists the change Jesus comes to bring. But if we allow John's call to repentance to sink into our souls, the Spirit of God can go to work within us to prepare the way for the transformation that Christ can bring. People whose lives are dominated by the power of sin can be transformed by the power of divine love into people whose lives are shaped into the likeness of Jesus Christ.

The gospel has good news for every rebellious child who needs to come home. We hear it in the song Zechariah sang at the birth of John the Baptist:

> By the tender mercy of our God,
>   the dawn from on high will break upon us,
> to give light to those who sit in darkness and in the shadow
>   of death,
>   to guide our feet into the way of peace. (Luke 1:78-79)

"The tender mercy of God" is what the runaway son found when he turned around and headed toward home. Jesus says that the elderly father ran, as fast as his arthritic legs could carry him, out to meet his son. He wrapped his tired, thin arms around the boy's sagging shoulders. He put a new coat on his son's sweaty back, and shoes on his blistered feet. Then he threw the biggest party the town had seen since New Year's Eve to welcome the lost son back home.

"The tender mercy of God" is God's unexpected forgiveness and grace, which we find precisely at the point where we realize that we have gone off in the wrong direction and turn around to come home.

I am richly blessed by the fellowship of eight other pastors who go away together at this time each year for a time of spiritual growth, supportive sharing, and enormous laughter. We've been together sixteen years now; we know the terrain of one another's souls pretty well. Last year one of the guys described the depression he was experiencing when he said, "I just don't feel at home." He named the specific things in his life that were causing him to feel disjointed, out of touch with himself and with God. He said he realized what was happening when he reread Robert Frost's poem "The Death of the Hired Man," in which the character Warren says,

Home is the place where, when you have to go there,
They have to take you in.

Warren's wife, Mary, responds,

I should have called it
Something you somehow haven't to deserve.
(*The Poetry of Robert Frost*, Holt, Rinehart
and Winston, 1969; page 38)

That's mercy. The tender mercy of God is the welcome we know we "somehow haven't to deserve"—in other words, it is a welcome we don't deserve, but one that is given to us anyway when we turn toward home. The awareness of that mercy began the dawning of a healing process for the depression in my soul-brother's life.

As I was writing this chapter, I recalled a personal note on a Christmas card. This note brought back to my mind the face of one particular person I knew, a man who is a lot like a lot of people I've known in every church I've served. Like the elder brother in Jesus' parable, he was a good boy. He grew up in the church. He did everything right. He became my friend. I was pained, though not entirely surprised, when in a very blatant manner, he turned to go his own way, acting in ways that were a defiant rejection of the faith in which he had been raised.

I stuck with him on his journey into the "far country." I journeyed with him to the place of repentance and return. It was a painful, difficult process. The wilderness road to repentance is so difficult, in fact, that many people simply refuse to take it. But this man did. He struggled through what he had done and the consequences of the choices he had made. In the wilderness of his soul, the tender mercy of God began to dawn upon him and set his feet on the way of peace. The Christmas card was the reminder of the way he experienced the mercy "you somehow haven't to deserve." This is the same tender mercy of God that awaits every wandering child who turns toward home.

One of my all-time favorite advertisements appeared in major newspapers across the country in 1976 while we were celebrating the bicentennial of the American Revolution. As I remember it, British Airways was attempting to entice the sons and daughters of the revolution—modern-day Americans—to visit Great Britain. The ad featured a rotund British character, appropriately dressed in a vested suit and bowler hat. Big Ben and the houses of Parliament were in the background.

The character was waving a tiny American flag and was announcing, beneficently, "Come home, America. All's forgiven."

The gospel invitation to every Christmas pilgrim is to come home. All is forgiven in the tender mercy of God. The dawn is about to break, and Jesus will lead our feet in the path of peace.

16
Come Home
to Bethlehem

ased on Luke 2:1-20

This world is wild as an old wives' tale,
And strange the plain things are,
The earth is enough and the air is enough
For our wonder and our war;
But our rest is as far as the fire-drake swings,
And our peace is put in impossible things
Where clashed and thundered unthinkable wings
Round an incredible star.
(G. K. Chesterton, "The House of Christmas,"
in *Modern British Poetry*)

A fellow pastor tells about a group tour of the Holy Land. One of the tour guides was a Bible scholar who knew all the latest results of archaeological analysis of the biblical sites. At their stop in Bethlehem, the guide informed the group that the site purported to be the birthplace of Jesus was clearly an eighteenth-century rebuilding of a third-century Roman structure. In cold, analytical terms, he went on to explain why it was very unlikely that this was actually the place where Jesus was born. As he was finishing up his lecture, another tour group crowded in beside them. The guide for the second group was clearly not a scholar and not very concerned about the historical accuracy of the site. He knelt on the floor in front of the group. With hushed reverence, in an almost mystical voice, he whispered, "Just think: This is the exact spot upon which our Lord was born, with angels singing and shepherds kneeling, and cattle lowing around him. This is the place where Mary wrapped him in swaddling cloths and laid him in a manger." It was at this point, the pastor said, that he overheard a member of his own group whisper wistfully, "I wish I were with them!"

We can analyze the scientific details of archaeology all year long, but on Christmas Eve there is something deep inside each of us that simply wants to be there at the place where Jesus was born. There is a homesickness in our souls to huddle in the stable with Mary and Joseph, to listen for the angels' song and to kneel with the shepherds before this child. Something in us wants to be there in Bethlehem.

The roads must have been crowded, the way roads are always crowded when oppressive powers cause forced migrations of refugee people. The Roman authorities demanded it. All of the people were to go to their ancestral homes. It was eighty miles from Nazareth to Bethlehem, and this was not an easy journey. This was not a trip you'd make if you didn't have to—certainly not a journey you would choose to make with a pregnant wife. There was only one reason Joseph went to Bethlehem. He was forced to go by the emperor's decree. He had to go to pay his taxes. I suspect he was just about as happy making that trip as we are when we head to the post office on April 15! But Joseph had no choice. He went to Bethlehem, Luke says, "because he was descended from the house and family of David" (2:4).

Bethlehem was not the place where Joseph lived, but it was the place he called "home." Bethlehem established his identity. It defined who he was.

In *The Longing for Home,* novelist and theologian Frederick Buechner reflects on his own journey home to God. He says that all of us live in two homes. The first is what he calls "the home we knew and will always long for, be homesick for." The second is "the home we dream of finding and for which we also long."

Deep within each of us there is the home we remember. Practically all of us can tell the story of the home in which we celebrated Christmas as a child, the place where we hung up our stocking, or the table around which we ate Christmas dinner. And every memory is unique. Some memories of home bubble over with effervescent joy; some are soaked with soul-numbing pain. Some memories we cherish; some we would prefer to forget. I suspect that most of our Christmas memories are like the steam pudding my mother taught me to make for Christmas. It blends a kitchen-counterful of ingredients into a mysterious, brown, cake-like climax to Christmas dinner that would seem strangely out of place any other day of the year. Similarly, each of us lives with memories that are a strange blend of laughter and tears, joy and pain. But what's there within each of us is the home we remember. It is the place from which we have come—the home that helped to define who we are.

Christmas Eve for me has a way of conjuring up the sights, sounds, and even the smells of a place to which I will never return. The home I remember was in a small town in Western Pennsylvania, about eighty miles north of Pittsburgh. If a heavy snowfall came in time for Christmas Eve, the tree-lined street where we lived took on a magical character. The cottony-white blanket muffled the sound of snow chains on passing cars in the days before snow-tread tires. The Christmas lights on the neighbor's shrubbery turned the snow into a patchwork quilt of glowing color. The decorations around the house were like old friends that we brought back out and put in the same places year after year.

This is the home to which I will never return. One of the houses in which I hung up my stocking now belongs to strangers who would probably be hard-pressed to recognize my name; and where the other house I lived in was, there is now a parking lot. But this is still the place I can never fully escape. It's the home that gave me my identity—and which, to some degree, made me who I am; the soul-home to which I cannot help returning if I am to understand the whole story of my life.

In the way that Joseph went home to Bethlehem, we need to make the soul-journey to the home we remember. We need to go to that place in our memory that defines the deepest realities of who we are; the deep inner core of our being where we hide the things that have hurt us in the past; the basement of our personality where we store the seeds of faith and hope. Like Joseph, we need to journey to our own Bethlehem, where we sing with Phillips Brooks, "The hopes and fears of all the years are met in thee tonight."

There's hardly a better time to make that journey home than on Christmas Eve. That is, after all, the way it happened for Ebenezer Scrooge in Charles Dickens's *A Christmas Carol*. Remember? On Christmas Eve, Scrooge took an unexpected and unwanted journey to the deepest places in his soul. He was forced to go to the places that defined who he had been, who he had become, and who he was becoming. It was only by going into the deep home within himself that he was able to receive the gift of new life on Christmas morning.

Joseph went home to Bethlehem, and there, Mary "gave birth to her firstborn son and wrapped him in bands of cloth, and laid him in a manger, because there was no place for them in the inn" (Luke 2:7). Of course, if they had stayed in Nazareth, the baby would have been born anyway; after all, babies have a way of doing that! But it is spiritually significant that Joseph went back to the place that defined his identity, and it was there that Jesus was born. If Jesus is to be born in us, he will be born at that same place within our souls.

Joseph went to Bethlehem because he had to; it was the home he remembered, the place with which he identified. The shepherds, on the other hand, went to Bethlehem because they wanted to. It was the home of which they dreamed.

Out there in the darkness, they received the good news that God's presence had intersected human history. God's life had become flesh in this baby. God's love had become a tangible reality in this child. And Luke's records that the shepherds "went with haste and found Mary and Joseph, and the child" (Luke 2:16). They went with the unbridled anticipation of children who run down the stairs on Christmas morning in hopes of finding the very thing for which they have dreamed. They went to Bethlehem out of the deepest longing of their homesick souls. And when they got there, they found Jesus.

We're talking about divine intervention here. This was nothing short of a divine intrusion into the old order, the old assumptions, the barren and tragic business-as-usual of a broken, hurting world. We're talking about the astounding good news that God has acted in human history. We're talking about one moment in time when all of the love and life of God was molded into human flesh and came forth from the womb of Mary. We call it the Incarnation. We dare to proclaim that this Jesus was exactly who the Gospels say he was: *Emmanuel*, which means "God is with us" (Matthew 1:23).

Charles Wesley declared the wonder of what the shepherds found in one of his Christmas carols, which hasn't appeared in American hymnals for nearly one hundred years.

Let earth and heaven combine,
   Angels and men agree,
To praise in songs divine
   The incarnate Deity,
Our God contracted to a span,
Incomprehensibly made man.

He deigns in flesh to appear,
   Widest extremes to join;
To bring our vileness near,
   And make us all divine:
And we the life of God shall know,
For God is manifest below.
               (from "Millennium,"
     Hymns on God's Everlasting Love, 1741)

A photograph of the United States Supreme Court, signed
by each justice, hangs on my office wall. It serves as a con-
stant reminder of one of my all-time favorite Christmas stories, a story about coming home. In 1989, Christmas Eve fell
on Sunday. Also in 1989 came the big freeze in Florida. We
awoke that Sunday morning in cold houses with frozen
water pipes because electrical power had been knocked out
across the central part of the state for most of the night.
When we arrived at the church, the sanctuary was so cold
that even people with no sense of pitch could tell that the
pipe organ was seriously out of tune. When the power went
out again during one of the hymns, the organ whined down
into cold silence, but we kept right on singing.

As we followed the choir procession into the sanctuary, I
noticed a dignified, gray-haired man in the aisle beside
Susie. Susie and William had joined our congregation during
the past year and had shared some of their story with me. I
knew that for both of them, coming to the church had been
a significant step of renewed faith after years of spiritual
separation and searching. In our congregation, they had
found their way home to God. I did not recognize the person

standing beside her, although his face looked vaguely familiar. When it came time to introduce guests, Susie stood up and said, "I want you to meet my father, Justice Harry Blackmun." I suddenly realized why he looked familiar. Susie's father was an active justice on the Supreme Court of the United States.

Susie's introduction of her father took us all by surprise, but none of us realized what a huge step it was for her to introduce him in church that day. Later, she told me the whole story, which she also wrote as a feature article in the *Orlando Sentinel.*

Susie was in college when President Richard Nixon appointed her father to the Supreme Court. The family's move to Washington, Watergate, the war in Vietnam, and the passions of the time ignited a major rebellion within Susie. Although her parents, Harry and Dottie Blackmun, were people of deep faith who had long been active in The United Methodist Church, Susie had already rejected the faith. Now she rejected her family and country as well. She sailed her way around the world, sometimes going for months without letting her parents know where she was.

Years passed. Susie married William and the couple had a daughter. As is often the case, grandchildren have a way of healing family relationships. That healing happened for Susie and her parents, except in regard to the church. Her father had simply given up on trying to get her back to the faith that meant so much to him. Susie told me that he could not have been more surprised if Santa Claus had actually dropped down the chimney than he was that Sunday morning over breakfast when she casually asked him, "Would you like to go to church with me?" When her father found out that it was a United Methodist church, for him that was even better! It was the best Christmas gift she gave him that year. The signed portrait of the Supreme Court that hangs on my office wall was Justice Blackmun's expression of gratitude for their reconciliation.

We celebrated Holy Communion in worship on that cold Sunday morning of Christmas Eve. After serving them bread and cup, I noticed that Susie and her father stayed at the altar rail for a long time, long enough for a Supreme Court justice to dry his tears before returning to his seat. When the newspaper published Susie's story, they titled it "The Long Journey Home." The introduction to the story read:

> In the church that day, Susie Blackmun held her father's hand at the Communion rail and watched him cry. Here was a towering figure of contemporary American history...standing in an Orlando church, crying joyfully at his reconciliation with a rebel daughter....It's certainly not a moment that Harry Blackmun was eager to share with the world....But this was his daughter's coming home. ("Florida Magazine," *Orlando Sentinel,* February 10, 1991, page 8)

The home for which we seek is that place where we know that we are one with God and one with each other. It's the family table where we are drawn together in the body and blood of Christ. It's that soul-place where we experience the peace on earth and goodwill to all that the angel promised. Frederick Buechner described it this way:

> To be homeless the way people like you and me are apt to be homeless is to have homes all over the place but not to be really at home in any of them. To be really at home is to be really at peace, and our lives are so intricately interwoven that there can be no real peace for any of us until there is real peace for all of us. (*The Longing for Home,* page 140)

We—all of us—live in two homes: the house we remember and the home we dream of. And the name of both is Bethlehem. Welcome home!